Corporate Guides to
Long - Range Planning

By Rochelle O'Connor

*A Research Report from The Conference Board's
Division of Management Research
Harold Stieglitz, Vice President*

About This Report

This report analyzes the guides, manuals and other documents corporations issue for developing long-range plans. More than half of the 83 company planners who contributed to this study also elaborated on their documents in interviews.

Part I of the report places planning guides in the context of the planning process and offers some general perspectives about them. It is based on the experiences and observations of the participating planners as revealed in interviews and letters.

Part II examines the types of written information supplied by headquarters as orientation to the company's planning process. It also includes a variety of formats and suggestions designed to aid the division manager to develop long-range plans.

Instructions and forms for preparing the specific elements of the division plan are covered in Part III: the executive summary; statement of mission, charter; the appraisal and situation analysis; objectives, goals; strategies; action programs; contingency planning.

The analysis of the planning guides is treated in a narrative manner, rather than as a summary of contents, for several reasons. Not every company provided a full set of its planning materials, and each company has its own unique approach toward guiding its divisions. While this study does not truly represent any one individual planning process, it does reflect the many current practices in corporate guidance for long-range planning.

Only those documents relating to the long-range planning activities of the participating companies — not the annual budget or short-term operating plans — are considered here.

The 83 companies contributing to the study represent 51 manufacturing companies; 10 banks or other financial institutions; 8 metals, mining and petroleum companies; 3 utilities; 3 insurance companies; and 8 miscellaneous industries. They range in annual sales from under $100 million to over $4 billion.

Contents

Exhibits

Foreword

THE CORPORATE PLANNING process that will best serve the needs of the 1970's is still evolving from its origins in the more prosperous 1960's. The aura of abundant resources that marked that decade has faded to the present reality of limited resources, and difficult decisions about their allocation.

These decisions, and the plans that prompt them, are based on both hard facts and on a vision of the future — on the strengths and weaknesses of the organization, on the most promising directions and goals, on the best routes toward accomplishing them.

The chief executive, whose broad views encompass the whole of the company, is the chief planner of the corporation. But planning responsibility ultimately involves all levels of management, particularly the managers of subsidiary units whose plans constitute the bulk of the corporate plan. Guiding them through the formulation of their plans is one of the most important tasks of the staff corporate planning function.

This latest Conference Board report on long-range planning is an examination of the documents, guides and instructions issued by corporations to help their managers develop the plans needed by top management. The ideal, of course, is to produce both good planning and good plans, useful to the managers as well as to top management.

The Conference Board is indeed grateful to the corporate planners who generously shared their companies' planning guides that serve as the basis of this study. Many of these individuals also offered explanatory comments and otherwise rounded out the subject in interviews.

This report was written by Rochelle O'Connor, Research Associate, under the guidance of James K. Brown, Director of Management Planning and Systems Research.

DAVID G. MOORE
Acting President

Part 1:
The Context of Planning

GOOD PLANNING FORMATS do not necessarily make for good planning or good plans. The documents studied for this report are all attempts — usually the most recent of several — to explain to the heads of divisions or subsidiaries what the corporate level of the organization wants from them. As expressions of the expectations of top management, corporate long-range planning guides are also intended to communicate concepts vital to effective planning, not merely instructions for filling in forms.

One of the dangers inherent in formalizing the planning procedure is the mistaking of form for substance. "The forms will not create the plan," cautions one company manual. Reporting formats must be recognized as summaries, or quantifications, of the results of strategic planning and not the planning itself, it goes on. The substance of planning may be stimulated by the format, many planners believe, but not replaced by it.

Several planners have noted that as a company's planning process matures, and managers become more skilled in developing long-range plans for their divisions, there is less adherence to the format. Some companies, as a matter of fact, have never formalized their planning programs, and claim they are satisfied with that approach. But other planners have commented that a less structured system has not worked well in their companies, frequently resulting in a lack of conformity that has made consolidation at the corporate level difficult or impossible.

Obviously, balancing the various elements that will produce the quality of planning wanted, in the form desired, is a task unique to each corporate organization. Written or unwritten, the company's planning philosophy and requirements must be conveyed to those responsible for leading their units. When a

The term "division," as used here, denotes a unit of the corporation that may actually be a subsidiary, group or company. Whatever it is called, it is a unit that submits a long-range plan to top corporate management. "Division" has been used to simplify what might otherwise prove to be confusing distinctions. Thus, references to "division manager" or "division plan" should be interpreted as the head of, or the plan of, a subsidiary unit of the organization.

While the "divisions" referred to in this report are usually line or operating divisions, some planning guides also refer to "staff divisions." These should be interpreted here as corporate staff units that serve in a support function and, like line divisions, are required to submit long-range plans to corporate headquarters.

company attempts to document the entire long-range planning process for its managers, it becomes a major corporate undertaking.

The Role of Documents

Planning documents have been described by some participants in this study as the "shell" of the real planning process, the "tip of the iceberg." In the narrowest sense, this is true. But, in a broader view, planning manuals and other guides can perform many more functions than simply outline corporate requirements, and many of them do.

Stimulate creative thinking. It is not easy to turn a busy manager away from his immediate day-to-day activities to focus on the longer view of his responsibilities. It is much less difficult for him to fill in boxes, or to delegate this function. For the most part, the corporate guides examined here are deliberate attempts to divert the manager from the nitty-gritty, to raise his sights from the annual budget, and to stir his imagination to dwell on the future of his unit. (This, of course, is one of the reasons many companies separate the long-range planning phase from the budgeting phase of the planning cycle.) Innovative presentation of corporate requirements, thoughtful sequencing of the development of the plan, and illustrative examples of what is desired are some of the ways that planners are encouraged to greater creativity.

Ease consolidation of the corporate plan. Assembling a total corporate plan from the input of the company's divisions is a monumental task for some firms. But to realize the final product, the culmination of the annual planning effort, all the bits and pieces must be fitted together, difficulties notwithstanding. The degree to which unit plans can be meaningfully consolidated is largely affected by the form in which the plans are presented to headquarters.

Companies that rely heavily on standard formats have little trouble in consolidating the total corporate plan. "Free-lance," creative planning, on the other hand, may prove unmanageable in the corporate scheme. Achieving a judicious balance between these two approaches is a continuous process for many corporate planning departments. Several companies that feel they are close to striking this balance are rewarded with creative divisional plans that are also easy to tie together.

Educate managers. Educating managers for the annual planning effort is an ongoing activity in most companies. For one thing, it generally takes more than one planning cycle for most divisional planners to achieve understanding of the process. For another, the process itself is likely to undergo revision as corporate needs change and experience suggests opportunities for improvement. Also, added to the readership of planning guides each year through executive turnover are those who have been newly promoted, appointed or inherited through corporate acquisition. Regardless of whether they have already participated to some

degree in the company's system, another company's system, or have never been called on before to plan, they must all be made familiar with *this* company's current planning procedure. To be sure, they are indoctrinated through meetings, seminars and personal contacts, but planning manuals and guides are the textbooks of the course.

Some of the manuals in this study have a strong pedagogical cast, as a matter of fact, and are used as training manuals in company planning seminars or management development programs. The education and training they provide apply not only to corporate planning, but also to related matters — the corporation's philosophy, businesses, policies, procedures.

Serve as a communication tool. Each year as planning documents are issued for the planning exercise, they say something about the company at that point. Previous plans have paid off, perhaps, and the stimulus of success is a rocket for the present year's plans. Or economic downturns have placed greater restrictions on some units; or missed opportunities have come to light. Whatever the message, the documents frequently perform vital communication functions between corporate and divisional levels. Where planning guides are able to establish a continuing dialogue between divisional management and the corporate planning department, such communication usually enhances the whole planning process.

Developing Guides

Because developing a corporate guide for long-range planning is not a one-shot event, it usually takes several planning cycles to arrive at a satisfactory format and to tailor a process to a company's unique specifications. Even if pretesting a new set of instructions in one or two divisions indicates that everything is on target, glaring mistakes can appear when applied to the whole organization. Unfortunately, "mistakes" in the planning format generally do not show up until the whole cycle is well under way or fully completed.

Outside Sources

Nevertheless, a start must be made somewhere. The planning documents submitted for this study are the products, initially at least, of several outside sources.

Consultants. A number of major management consultants provide planning services, and there are also specialized planning consultants. Of the companies cooperating in this study, a number have engaged consultants to set up their planning process, and some of the planning guides submitted show striking similarities. Planners who have used consultants are satisfied with the results in general, but most have instituted changes since inception of the process. Some admit to paring down the amount of detail initially required, or otherwise retaining the basic planning approach but making other changes. Other company planners have investigated the approaches of several consultants and selectively adopted from each approach the parts they found useful.

Courses, seminars. Advanced business courses and management development programs have provided the foundations of several planning guides studied in this report. Corporate planners or members of their top management teams have attended such educational programs and brought the fundamentals of long-range planning back to the company, where they have found expression in manuals.

Other companies. A major influence in the formulation of corporate planning guides is the experience of other companies. During the normal course of conducting business or attending meetings, planners exchange experiences of mutual concern. It is not uncommon for them to exchange planning manuals as well, or to extend the courtesy of fully briefing one another on planning problems. The documents in this report show evidences of these exchanges.

Another way in which companies influence one another's planning procedures and planning guides is by hiring executives of other companies. Such appointees apply what they have learned in their former positions to their new firms.

Planning literature. A relative newcomer in the business management field, long-range planning was not part of the curriculum for older executives who later found it necessary to educate themselves in the subject. Still an evolving discipline, and replete with unsolved problems, planning is receiving the attention of scholars and publishing in the field is extensive. Most planners soon become acquainted with the literature.

Other Influences

The design of the planning system bears the imprint of qualities unique to the company. Most apparent, of course, is the size and variety of business or businesses of the organization, but there are less obvious factors that strongly influence how long-range planning operates in all companies. The style of management and the company traditions that govern its approach to planning play a large part in how the procedures are implemented.

Size and variety of business. Size alone does not imply complexity in the planning system. Some very large companies in extractive industries, for example, have a small number of products or limited markets. The type of input they require from their divisions is relatively simple. "After all," one planning executive has stated, "we are all oil men here [at headquarters] and are always in touch with the situation." Highly diversified companies, on the other hand, must often sift through a multitude of different kinds of businesses with completely different environments. In order to make sound decisions, management requires much more background data from divisional plans.

Dealing with a diversity of businesses can pose problems for corporate planners, and they employ different methods to cope with the situation. One approach is to issue a single, generalized document of instructions that each unit can adapt to its needs. This allows the divisions a fair amount of leeway.

A second approach is to issue distinctive procedures for each division. (Many firms have different formats for line and staff units, too.)

In this case, there are certain standard portions that apply to all units, but special forms for the different businesses. Attempts are made, of course, to develop formats that can be conformed at headquarters.

There are also those who cannot see imposing any format at all. "To institute a formal format for different types of businesses would be sacrificing needed flexibility for uniformity," insists the planning director of a pharmaceutical firm that issues no planning guides. It allows the divisions to express their plans in the manner they consider most appropriate.

In general, the spectrum of industries represented in this report shows no dramatic differences in the basic elements of their divisional or subsidiary plans. But, of course, each type of industry is likely to have a distinctive weighting of individual components. Financial and other nonmanufacturing companies are more concerned with manpower and the number, size and location of offices, say, than manufacturing firms that tend to concentrate on capital appropriations. Food processors build crop data into their analyses; railroads may focus on cost reduction or safety programs; and many heavily regulated industries must foresee legislation that will seriously affect their operations. Utilities, of course, have concerns peculiar unto themselves.

Style of management. There is no doubt, according to the executives interviewed, that the style of the chief executive is a determinant of the style of planning at the company: His vision of the company exerts a strong influence on the planning program. Top management has defined *needs* that must be met. Top management, however, also has *wants*, perhaps less insistently articulated, that planning directors are sensitive to. Some company heads make demands that shape the system, or display personal characteristics that profoundly affect the planning process.

Catering to the preferences of top management may impose certain kinds of planning formats. For instance, some chief executives want numbers, others want prose; some want charts, others tables. Some planners speak of chief executives who read through all the divisional plans in their entirety; others, of top men who display impatience at "going through the stuff they already know."

One firm has a chairman who wants concise, brief reports — an executive summary and "no garbage" — while the president delights in all the details and tables that are supplied. Another company sees itself as "a group of entrepreneurs" and does not use any specific documents in requesting information from the field.

"Style" also extends to the manner in which directions are given. Although the guides all request common types of information on very similar subjects, they reveal distinctiveness in the tone in which they ask for it, and in the manner in which they want it presented. Some guides figuratively bark out "drill-sergeant" orders, while others offer surprisingly gentle "suggestions." Some are didactic, but some are a bare outline of minimum requirements.

Some planning guides acknowledge and encourage the individual styles of divisional executives. "Every divisional business plan format is different," says the planning executive of a chemical manufacturer, because each division manager has his own style, ideas and technique for presenting his long-range plans to management. In an oil company, substantial latitude in designing formats and in using forecasting techniques is also permitted. "Rigid, formal documentation channels, rather than stimulates, thinking," the planning director believes. Another company planner would rather have his managers think than "just fill in a form." He points out, too, that a lot can be learned about managers this way.

Another advantage to this approach, according to some planners, is that the written instructions need not be constantly revised to maintain an up-to-date manual if strict formalities are not laid down. This is pertinent because recasting the planning process each year to eliminate old problems or otherwise meet new requirements often brings a toll of new problems.

Degree of Structure and Flexibility

Closely tied to the style of management — permissive, authoritarian, informal, formal — is the degree of structure built into the planning formats. A decision that must be made early in developing a planning guide is the degree of uniformity needed or desired from organization units. The need for establishing a sound trade-off between ease of consolidating divisional plans and possible restrictions of creative ideas has already been mentioned.

Financial formats tend to be fairly rigid in all organizations because figures must be consolidated or fed into computers. Sometimes these schedules fall prey to the tyranny of the form in which data are available in the firm. If they have been developed to fit regular accounting procedures, not all the statistics provided are needed or wanted for planning purposes; others that are needed or wanted may not be provided. In short, function sometimes follows form.

Requests for nonfinancial material are more open to flexibility and permissiveness. A number of guides encourage the managers to modify suggested formats to suit the needs of the unit if that will lead to better content and substance in their responses. Environmental assumptions handed down from the corporate level, particularly, are often open to modification (see Part III).

In another decision, implicit in the preparation of the planning guides, a company affirms its choice of emphasis: planning or plans, although one need not exclude the other.

The *plans* emphasis is marked by explicit instructions and a logical, sequential preparation. The manager who is doing the planning is led from one segment of the plan to another until he has completed the entire exercise. A drawback cited by one planner is that such a stylized approach can produce a certain amount of redundancy and disjointedness in the plan. For example, the disposition of a weak product announced in the strengths and weaknesses section cannot be completely followed through until objectives and strategies are presented. Such a format may be restrictive but it allows for easier organization of plans and relating of inputs to one another.

With the *planning* emphasis, one often finds deliberate generalization or vagueness of instructions to achieve two objectives that further the firm's dedication to sound divisional planning. When the planning policy of the firm is to promote communication, the paucity of definition provokes questions and an ensuing dialogue between divisional executives and the corporate planning department. This leads, it is argued, to a second objective — enhancing planning skills. Thus several companies make sure that their written instructions are not totally self-explanatory so that interpretation must be obtained through personal contact. They feel more thoughtfulness goes into the planning with such discussion.

Most of the planning executives participating in the study applaud less rigid documentation. This less-structured approach is encouraged, they indicated in interviews, regardless of how formalized the planning guides and manuals may appear. And one study participant stresses that it is important not to require exhibits in the planning documentation for which managers cannot see the need.

Regardless of the degree of structure in the planning format, the uncertainty of the economy has underscored the need for flexibility in planning procedures. Several planners feel it is necessary to be able to make quick changes: They believe that assumptions must be turned over fairly frequently, or that in-house simulation models are necessary to plug in changes at any time during the year. "Five-year plans are not contracts," states the planning director of an automotive firm, "they are already obsolete when written."

Changing the Planning Process — and the Guides

If any insight emerges from the planning experiences of the companies participating in this report, it is that most company planning programs are in a state of constant change. Many have undergone numerous minor changes, and some have experienced major upheavals during the past decade, when most of the systems studied here were established. With these changes have come changes in the planning guides.

Not only is each company's experience with formal planning unique, but also each reacts to its experience in a distinctive manner. Hence it is not surprising to find changes being made in one company that are diametrically opposite to those being made in another company. Whereas one company may be imposing a longer interval between the strategic planning and budgeting phases of the planning cycle, another may have just decided to move them closer together. One company may hand down divisional objectives while another may have recently switched to a bottom-up process.

A not uncommon company practice is change to stimulate alertness. In one pharmaceutical company, for example, instructions and timetables are varied from year to year in a deliberate attempt to maintain organizational awareness and involvement in the planning process. "As soon as it settles into a routine . . . the system will lose its effectiveness and will be delegated to third-rate staff people filling in forms," asserts the planning director. However, most of the changes that are made in the planning process or format are designed to react to new situations.

Changes in the Economy, the Industry, the Company

In many firms, the final planning process developed and rode the crest of the ebullient 1960's, but the climate of the 1970's has forced their managements to reappraise and rearrange these processes. Forecasting the future environment has become even more perplexing, and even smaller companies are finding themselves affected directly by global issues.

Three Banks

Three large banks participating in this study reflect different individual approaches to the long-range planning process and the related corporate guides.

Bank A has a formal, highly structured planning procedure and format. Contained in a 123-page looseleaf binder devoted to the planning system is the statement of the bank's philosophy that the successful long-range planning program should be "...formal in nature requiring documentation not only of the plans submitted by the divisions and subsidiaries, but also of the policies and procedures to be followed in the planning process...."

Bank B issues its planning guides in 12 terse pages of complete instructions with illustrative examples plus a small appendix.

Bank C claims it is an "informal organization" without heavily structured guidelines. It has avoided standard formats because it believes each division is different from every other.

In the aftermath of unforeseen threats and missed opportunities, many companies are altering some aspects of their planning systems and formats. Such attempts usually aim to avoid surprises or to allow a faster response to sudden or unexpected change.

Contingency, alternative or supplementary planning, while not highly visible in the manuals under study, is being seriously considered by many of the planning executives interviewed. Alternative scenarios are being offered or requested in several companies. A number of companies have found it necessary to add instructions on how to account for the inflation factor in financial forecasts. An oil company makes changes in its forms annually to include new factors that might have an impact on the company.

Several companies report the introduction of a "preliminary plan" before submission of the final plan. While this is frequently done to facilitate top management review meetings, it is also a deliberate attempt to hold off as long as possible "casting in concrete" plans based on assumptions made in a quickly changing environment.

Another change occasioned by the altered business milieu of the past few years is the addition of product-analysis exercises to divisional planning activities. A number of companies have found that managing a diverse portfolio of enterprises in leaner times requires more extensive information and evaluation than they had previously sought.

Changes also have had to be made in the planning process for companies that have more recently experienced growth and expansion. At least one organization — a farm machinery manufacturer — found that its former informal planning structure was inadequate to meet the demands of its new global status. The planning director is now in the process of writing guides to strategies — "the company way" — for the new companies that have come under its aegis. On the other hand, as a company's planning program gets more established, and division executives become more experienced in planning, less direction from the corporation may be needed.

New Key Executives

A prime agent of change, of course, is a new chief executive, a new management team, or a new planning director. They frequently bring with them fresh insights and aspirations that are relayed to the planning process. Also, the transition of power to a younger generation of managers is often the setting for a more sophisticated approach to planning.

To illustrate: The previous decade's acquisitions have been the cause of considerable managerial turnover in acquired companies, according to the planning officer of a large corporation. The entrepreneurs who had built up the acquired businesses either retired or lost intrest in the operation within a few years after the acquisitions. Their successors were largely professional managers, who asked for more guidance from the corporation in the planning function and in the running of the business. This

necessitated adapting the planning procedures to the new needs.

A West Coast bank reports that after many cycles of a bottom-up planning process, a new chief operating officer — the president — demanded a top-down approach. After a few years, and just as the bank decided to reintroduce more bottom-up input, a new president was appointed whose views on planning are not yet known. Thus the rapid turnover of presidents has led to a succession of changed formats, none of which has been able to complete its course of development.

A new corporate planning director is apt to take a completely fresh look at the previous incumbent's planning process and institute changes. One reports that, after one or two cycles of the planning process, he posed pertinent questions to division managers and made drastic changes in line with the answers he received.

Sometimes the failure or inadequacy of a planning system leads a company to engage a consultant to revamp the process and supporting guides. The influence of a consultant is often tantamount to that of a new key executive.

"Fine Tuning" the System

Minor adjustments can smooth the rough edges that appear in any business endeavor. In planning, such nuisances become apparent during the course of a planning cycle or immediately afterwards, and attempts to correct them are designed to correct specific malfunctions.

The burdens placed on the various organizational levels during the planning process are often the source of the complaints that lead to adjustments. When top management in one company was taxed by planning review sessions, the dates for submission of divisional plans were staggered to ease the load the following year.

Another company found that its operating managers disliked the six months' lapse between strategic planning and budgeting phases because it entailed a completely new effort on their part. The company moved to a three months' lapse between these two parts of the planning process, thus eliminating the "whole new ball game" aspect that upset the managers.

Occasionally several levels of the corporate structure can benefit from an adjustment of planning requirements. The search for good summary forms, for example, is one that preoccupies planning departments, both for themselves and for busy top executives. Corporate staff planners usually have to summarize voluminous division plans before presentation to top management.

Many minor changes are made in planning systems in the cause of simplification. This appears to be a never-ending effort of corporate planners. But streamlining some aspects of the system is not always possible. While the accounting system may not furnish exactly the information that is needed or wanted, for example, there is strong resistance in many firms to changing it.

The introduction of computer facilities or financial models, however, has made it necessary for several companies to revise their guides to accommodate these new developments. Some, indeed, have devised complete sets of instructions on using the new facilities for managers — even separate supplements to the planning manuals are reported.

The Problem of Plan Size

"Everybody wants to write *Gone with the Wind*," complains the planning director of a large publishing concern. This terse comment sums up a big — literally — problem of many planning departments.

The amount of plan documentation that has swamped so many company managements has led to planning system renovations to obtain only the *minimum* amount of information needed to make decisions. Although large amounts of data are needed to formulate plans, many managements have questioned the necessity of submitting all of these data to the top level of the organization. A large diversified company prefaces its manual with the observation that the documents submitted reflect "only a distillation of the detailed analysis and planning which must be carried on within the division to develop a meaningful, realistic plan. . . ."

Most of the companies that have taken steps to cut down on the bulk of submitted divisional plans have done so on a piecemeal basis. Some have completely revamped their planning instructions and guides to produce plans of more manageable dimensions.

Sometimes such revised planning manuals are themselves rather bulky documents, and the consternation of the top corporate executive on receiving a 300-page division plan must be matched to the dismay of the division executive who receives a 100-page volume of corporate planning instructions. But planners who have revised planning guides insist that it is necessary to spell out completely and fully the new directions and size limitations to emphasize the conciseness and brevity wanted.

As already suggested, the burden of overlong division plans falls on the corporate planning department, as well as on top management. The corporate planner and his staff are often under severe time limitations when summarizing and filtering out voluminous division plans. Experience has taught them to expect more information than is needed and that they must reduce the bulk presented to corporate management. This is a spur to attempts to cut down on the size of plans presented to them.

Some Solutions

While some planners have hacked away piecemeal at various portions of overabundant plans, many have resorted to more radical measures to bring down the bulk of the documents submitted. For instance, some companies no longer require all of their business units to present complete long-range plans. One manufacturer that has placed all its business units and profit centers into different types of reporting categories requires written plans from only some of them. The others are encouraged to prepare plans for their own internal use, but to provide only financial estimates to the corporate level.

Another company manual has a section on business codes that defines the reporting documentation required of each business unit. Some are asked to provide complete business plans; others need furnish only background data and profile summaries, or only operating budgets.

One of the most successful ways of limiting the size of the divisional documentation of the long-range plan is simply that: placing size limitations on each element of the plan and on the plan as a whole. The documents studied in this report show numerous instances of constraints on the length of different portions of the plan. These injunctions may be worded emphatically and specifically, detailing page size, spacing and margins, number of paragraphs. Another method of handling this is to devise a specialized format that circumscribes the amount of data that can be offered.

One organization that restudied its requirements and revised its planning manual to accommodate them claims that the new format should produce a 90 percent reduction in the volume of plans. The text of each business unit's strategic plan is not allowed to exceed 10 to 12 pages. Other companies have also set page restrictions on their plans, making it clear that they are interested only in key actions to

The Best Years for Planning

It usually requires several cycles to tailor a planning process to fit a company, most planners agree.

According to one bank planner, it takes five years "to get mileage" out of the planning system — to educate managers in planning and for them to learn how to plan. The first four or five years, he claims, are "pony shows" of extravagant claims and plans. Then everyone settles down to valuable planning. Another planner terms the first five years the "gestation" period.

But, according to the planning head of an industrial machinery products manufacturer, the first and second planning cycles for a manager show the most original thinking and the most serious involvement. Thereafter, the planning becomes a maintenance function that does not sustain his interest.

achieve strategies on a priority basis, not operating details.

A number of instructions even limit the number of objectives, or strategies and the like, that a division may submit. While most experienced division heads avoid excesses in these elements of their plans, persons newly appointed to these positions can produce surprises — as can a new planning system. One study contributor cited an overzealous division manager's internal appraisal: "He listed 27 weaknesses!"

The elimination of some data requirements is a sure way to decrease the volume of a plan. And many companies that have taken close looks at what they were getting found a number of places where material could be omitted without seriously affecting the plan proper. Many companies have simply dropped their requirements for certain exhibits or tables. Some have tried to devise formats that would include only the necessary data.

A new planner in a glass products company, on examining the planning system he had inherited and the results it produced, was able to eliminate from the material submitted to top management the descriptions of the market, the competition and the strengths and weaknesses sections of the divisional plan.

An obvious way of reducing plan size, of course, is eliminating plan submission altogether. Although none of the companies studied here has done that, some are not demanding full-scale plans every year. They may ask for plans from half the units in the organization one year; the rest in intermediate years. Or they may request only updates of the previous year's plan, or only changes that will have a major impact on the long-range plan.

Some changes that are made in the planning process achieve a reduction in plan size as a by-product. For instance, those companies that are shortening their time frames because they feel that projections beyond the next two or three years are not worthwhile find that this appreciably diminishes the amount of data submitted. An emphasis on strategy, rather than numbers, also seems to cut the bulk of plans in many companies.

A more complicated method of dealing with the problem of size has been tried by a leisure products company. It provides specific tailor-made instructions for each business unit and profit center on what forms to complete, what major product lines to cover, what financial information to provide, and what data are necessary for the review meeting with the top level of the corporation.

Problems with Strategy

"The format is fine but . . . " For many companies, getting managers to do good strategic planning is evidently beyond the power of written corporate guides to planning. In fact, a common complaint of many planning directors is that division managers do not address themselves to the most relevant issues, the issues of strategy. Even though all the right slots in the forms have been filled in, and a corporate plan can be consolidated, the key issues and threats have not been confronted. The biggest defect of past planning efforts, according to a West Coast bank, "has been the failure to describe the path we will take and not just the results we want."

This problem is not easily resolved. It is one of the continuing challenges of educating personnel in planning. Some guides incorporate "good" examples of strategies to illustrate the type of thinking they want, but illustrating the concepts apparently does not provide the basics of strategic planning.

One planner, who claims the strategic section is the most difficult to deal with, reports that he has taught his managers to analyze strategy by focusing on growth, and then thinking of the support for that growth: personnel, facilities, systems, and so on. The planning head of a publishing company, who had a hard time explaining the differences between objectives and strategies to division planners, says: "I told them that objectives meant the profits they were going to make for the company. Everything else was strategy."

Many companies try to elicit more creative strategic thinking in long-range plans by separating it from financial projections or commitments. The two cannot be done simultaneously, according to many planners. Some planning systems even encourage plans to be submitted for discussion without a commitment to premature figures.

A container company says it is de-emphasizing financial implications of the long-range plan and focusing on the value of building a base of facts on the environment. Even though the numbers in a five-year forecast may not be so reliable, it considers an updated fact base a valuable tool for the formulation of strategy.

Most of the planners participating in this study are convinced that, regardless of how poorly line managers develop strategy, they are still the ones who must do the planning if they are to be committed to the plan. Doing this at the corporate level for the divisions does not work, it is claimed, because this would crimp the prerogative of divisional executives in running their businesses.

Part 2:
Orientation to Company Planning

THE BULK OF CORPORATE planning guides is given over to suggestions and instructions pertaining to order, content and arrangement of divisional plans. But invariably these guides also include material that is intended to stimulate and assist divisional executives and to enable them to see how their efforts fit into the firm's planning system as a whole — material that, to put it another way, gives them a framework for planning. This material embraces such subjects and issues as:

. The need for and purposes of planning.

. Salient information about the planning process — notably the planning calendar and the agenda of various planning meetings held during the course of the planning cycle.

. Aids to planning — definitions of vital terms, "how to do it" suggestions and illustrations, references to relevant literature.

In addition, information is often provided about the company as a whole — its mission, its objectives, and its goals.

Not every guide, of course, treats every one of these subjects.

Reasons for Planning

If, as seems to be a widespread article of faith, the reasons for planning need to be broadcast frequently and forcefully to the managers of a corporation, planning guides provide a useful and convenient medium for the message. In this context, their aim is to help orient division managers to the planning process to which they are asked to make a significant contribution. A number of companies introduce their guides with a background piece on the need for, purposes of, and results expected from the planning process.

A food processor's manual lists, for instance,

the chief factors that have impelled it to adopt a formal planning system:

". The increasingly complex management task of running a large decentralized and geographically dispersed business organization.

". The ever-increasing pace of change in the many external factors which affect our business.

". The growing pressures from changes in the marketplace and from increasingly aggressive and sophisticated competition.

". The limitations of our financial, technical and management resources.

". The lead time and growing complexities of many key business decisions (e.g., product development, facilities utilization, management development).

". And, finally, the very important need to communicate policies and plans between world headquarters and company management and to large numbers of company employees to enlist their support and gain their commitment to the effort to achieve company goals."

A larger view of the planning exercise is offered by one manufacturer:

"The primary purpose of strategic planning is to develop and annually update a frame of reference for making current decisions which are consistent with long-range development strategies and are steps in the evolution of the business toward the achievement of the long-range objectives. The purpose is not to make future decisions now."

A bank makes this statement: "The end purpose of planning is not to produce another document, but to draw agreement from the management levels as to what they will be trying to accomplish over the planning horizon."

In explaining that a newly adopted strategy-center planning program is designed to develop

(1) a comprehensive, up-to-date explicit statement of company strategy, and (2) a system to relate the company strategy to programs and objectives that can be acted upon at the division level and below, one apparel company's manual states:

"Within these broad boundaries are a number of important secondary objectives of the strategic planning program:

". Provide the company's managers with a common planning language and system of planning logic and a durable process which can continue to be applied in future business analyses.
". Establish a framework for viewing the company and its components and for structuring the decision-making process.
". Provide a uniform basis for constructive evaluation among divisions.
". Supplement existing controls over asset allocation.
". Help managers develop a more comprehensive understanding of the dynamics of their business."

The need for dialogue between top management and subsidiary management is explained in yet another company's manual:

"[The company's] size and diversity of businesses make clear communications of objectives and expectations between the executive office and the groups and business units indispensable. The strategic plan is the means for accomplishing this communication: it is the vehicle for a dialogue between the executive office and operating management. Ideas are to be exchanged in the development of key objectives and strategies which will assure that each business unit operates as an integral part of [the company], maximizing its contribution to [the company] — not necessarily independently maximizing for its own development. The approved formal strategic plan becomes the final agreed-upon operating guide for the business units."

One of the benefits expected from a formal planning program is a system that is the means for consolidating division plans into a cohesive corporate plan. One firm cites the necessity to "coordinate and integrate all these decentralized plans to assure that they are consistent with each other; that conflicts are recognized and resolved."

The material orienting the division manager to the company's planning process frequently defines his role as planner. An aluminum fabricator's manual, for example, states that ". . . planning for a corporate segment can be done best by those familiar with its problems, who are responsible for taking action and achieving results in that segment." Or, to quote a bank's manual: "Effective planning cannot be done to or for an organization; it must be done by the responsible managers. . . . Planning is not done by staff groups, but rather through the participation of all levels of management."

A company that has recently inaugurated a new planning program describes its "Corporate Strategy Guideline Statement" as a "cornerstone of the strategic planning program." It goes on to explain that the statement "sets forth the basic environmental assumptions to be used in the planning effort, the basic role of both corporate and division management in guiding the course of the company, a set of objectives and policies for the corporation, and basic strategies to be employed by the company.

"It is recognized that any statement is a static document while the planning process itself is dynamic in nature. Therefore the Corporate Strategy Guideline is both a beginning and an end. We will use it as a beginning to initiate and guide the planning process; at the same time we recognize the need to incorporate in it the lessons learned during each planning cycle, as well as any differences in our outlook for the future. Thus the incorporation of feedback into our guidelines also marks an end in the planning cycle and an important goal of the planning process."

Purpose of the Planning Manual

Most introductions to planning manuals also state the purpose of the planning manual itself.

"The purpose of this document is to summarize the major planning elements carried out within [the company] to serve as a guide to both corporate and company executives in planning future business growth. It is intended that this material will:

"1) Develop a *uniform understanding* among key executives of the major planning activities and responsibilities at [the company] and how the various elements of planning fit together.

"2) Describe for all key managers in the company our *basic approach* to planning and outline the activities necessary to get the job done.

"3) Serve as a *training guide* to assist in the development of management skills of managers who must participate in the process."

The Planning Process

To gain full support and cooperation for the planning effort, a number of companies try to explain the workings of the process. This shows the division manager how his unit fits into the planning procedures, and how the total corporate plan is developed.

The Planning Calendar, Flow Charts

Appended to the chief executive's announcement of a new planning cycle, or else holding a separate position of its own, is the calendar of events associated with the annual planning effort.

Time schedules for the issuance of guidelines, submission of plans, review meetings, and approvals are usually meticulously worked out to allow for the intricate timing involved in putting a corporate long-range plan together. Time must be allowed for divisional input to be assembled and analyzed, for plans to be revised, and for documents to pass from one organizational level to another. All divisional plans have to be consolidated, with conflicts resolved, before the plans are finally approved and the next phase — near-term planning or budgeting — gets under way.

Calendars vary in the amount of their detail, but they always give deadlines for submission of the divisional plans. Some calendars list individual responsibilities for each step in the process.

Flow charts or other graphic presentations of the planning system are often extremely complex. But there is a good reason for includ-

Exhibit 1: Strategic Planning Model — A Publishing Company

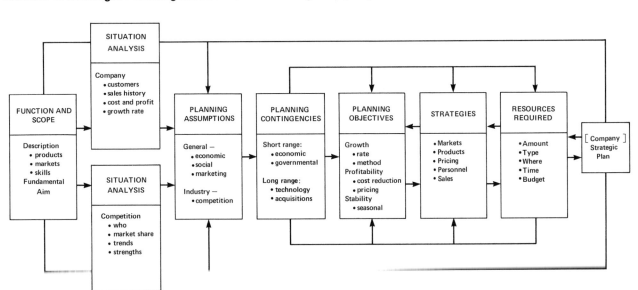

Exhibit 2: Strategic Plans Approval and Control System — A Financial Services Company

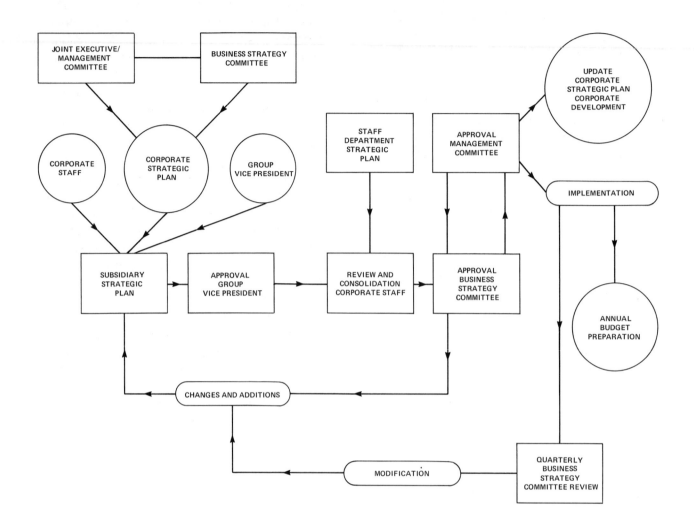

ing this type of material in the documents — their educational value carries a strong impact. Such documents display the interactions among different levels and functions of the company, how the planning sequences work, and how the consolidated plan evolves. Further, they often illustrate the feedback process fostered by a good planning system — an element sometimes doubted by frustrated managers.

Meetings, Reviews

A number of long-range planning guides include requirements for planning meetings and review sessions. Not all guides carry the dates for these meetings, presumably because some

flexibility in scheduling is preferred to a rigid timetable developed more than a year in advance. In this circumstance such announcements and agenda are issued separately and closer to the meeting date.

The most typical meeting covered in long-range documents is the planning review meeting at which the unit manager presents his plan to corporate top management. This is a red-circle date and some guides issue extensive directions for preparing for it. The purpose of these review sessions, in the words of one manual, is to ensure that: "(1) all division activities are integrated, (2) overall objectives are attainable, and (3) the plan is reasonable."

Exhibit 3: Planning Timetable — A Food Processor

	Timetable	Notes
I. Competitors/Assumptions/Potential/Case Sales	11/25-1/10 (7 weeks)	This first step should be started right after the profit plan is finalized.
II. Capabilities	12/16-1/10 (3 weeks)	This should be completed prior to organization plans and capital budgets.
III. Crop Data	12/23-1/17 (4 weeks)	This allows one week to convert case sales to tons. Data Processing program should be ready.
IV. Case Sales by Plant	1/13-1/17 (1 week)	Industrial Engineering should be alerted so that this step is started right after I.
V. Organization	1/20-2/14 (4 weeks)	Must follow case sales per plant. G.O. personnel should be determined early.
VI. Capital Budgets	1/20-2/21 (5 weeks)	Starts right after case sales by plant.
VII. Plant Strategies	1/20-2/21 (5 weeks)	Should be closely coordinated with capital budget.
VIII. Expense Budgets	2/10-3/7 (4 weeks)	
IX. Other Expense	2/24-3/7 (2 weeks)	Must follow capital budgets and organization plans.
X. Income Statement/New Business	3/10-3/28 (3 weeks)	Must follow expense and other expense. Data Processing program should be ready.
XI. Performance Data/Industry Assumptions/Strategies/Projects	3/10-4/4 (4 weeks)	Should follow semiannual project report. Economist's report should precede.
XII. Other Financial Objectives	3/31-4/11 (2 weeks)	Must follow income statement.
XIII. General Objectives	4/14-4/18 (1 week)	Must follow other financial objectives.
XIV. Corporate Summary	4/21-4/26 (1 week)	Must follow general objectives.

Exhibit 4: Planning Cycle — A Manufacturer of Industrial Products

January

- Develop or review charter and fields of interest.
- Identify key segments of the business. Products, markets or a combination of the two should be placed into business units.

February

- Begin preparation of capital expenditure requirements for next three years as per SPI C-1. *Due April 1.*
- Prepare fact sheet on each business unit.
- Decide on long-term key objectives for each business unit.

March

- Develop alternate strategies for each business unit. Analyze, discuss and review each.
- Review long-term action plans and key issues developed last summer.
- Review and complete (if not already done) the 5-year financial schedules prepared last fall.

April

- Submit capital expenditure plans for next three years. *Due April 1.*
- Decide on recommended strategy for each business unit.
- Compile and send Strategy Review Book to Plan Review Committee. *Due April 10.*
- Spring plan review meetings to discuss and decide on business unit strategies. *April 18-23.*

May

- Review of capital expenditure requests.
- Receive key issues developed at plan review meetings.
- Decide on final strategy for each business unit.
- Begin solicitation and sorting of planning issues.

June

- Receive short-term economic forecast.
- Receive preliminary capital expenditure allotment for following year.
- Decide on key issues for which action plans need to be developed.
- Begin development of action plans.

July

- Receive long-term economic forecast.
- Develop action plans.

Exhibit 4 (continued)

August

- Finalize action plans.
- Initiate work on next year's budget.
- Develop 5-year financial schedules.
- Receive final short-term economic forecast.

September

- Finalize budget and 5-year financial schedules. *Due September 10.*
- Finalize key objectives for next year. *Due September 10.*
- Compile and send planning book which includes objectives, action plans, key issues, budgets and 5-year financial schedules to Plan Review Committee. *Due September 16.*
- Fall plan review meetings to review and discuss next year's plans and budgets. *September 24-26.*

October

- Finalize budgets.
- Finalize capital expenditures.

November

- Board of directors approval of budgets.
- Board of directors approval of capital expenditures.

The preparation expected of managers for these oral and visual presentations may be detailed and rigid, or may entail only the exposition of the executive summary of their plans. The time allotted for each unit — depending on its size and complexity and the firm's style — may vary from 20 minutes to two days.

Managers may be given a great deal of freedom in presenting their submissions, so long as they offer the information required. "Come prepared with substantive materials for aid in fielding appropriate questions concerning trends, etc.," advise a grain company's instructions. Most companies want much of the material in some sort of graphic form — charts, graphs, slides and the like.

Other Features

Other features of the planning process are covered in some planning guides, depending on how thoroughly the firm wishes to spell out the whole system. If the issued documents are assembled into a procedures book, all aspects may be described in detail.

Individual responsibilities. Individual planning responsibilities may be outlined in connection with elements of the plan and due dates.

Controls and monitoring. Some manuals set forth these procedures as an extension of the planning process, but they are usually considered apart from the planning system.

Types of plans. Many manuals and instructions attempt to describe and explain the different types and levels of plans used in the company and their relationships. They include: preliminary or final; group or division; strategic or operating; and so on.

Budgeting and short-range planning instructions. The gamut of the company's planning may be contained in one volume.

Special company programs. Programs adopted by a company that are considered to impinge on the planning process, or to be directly related to it, are described in several sets of guides. Examples: management for results, management by objectives.

Codes. Business unit codes of the company are another common item found in the more far-ranging documents, as well as other specialized codes that may affect planning procedures.

Special accounting and financial instructions. Apart from the instructions for preparing the regular financial forms for the plan, many manuals include special sections of financial forms and instructions for them. Several also give detailed instructions for computing required data.

Other planning-related procedures. Other planning-related procedures, described in some planning manuals, include: capital project appropriation requests; asset disposal or approval requests; project priority reporting systems; EDP steering committee procedures.

Aids to Planning

The overall planning process is designed to enhance decision making by top management and specific planning procedures are developed to further that end. More specifically, they are geared to produce divisional plans in a form that will facilitate consolidation, review and ultimate approval.

But making things easier at the top may create hardships at lower levels. Thus it is that many guides contain sections aimed at alleviating these hardships.

Advice and Suggestions

Encouragement and advice run through the pages of quite a number of the manuals and documents studied. Almost all offer the services of the planning staff and invite questions and discussion, either in the transmittal letter or elsewhere. Other corporate staff sources that may be called on for assistance are also usually listed.

The Kick-Off Letter

The transmittal of the guidelines for each new planning cycle is almost always accompanied by a letter or memorandum — from the chief executive or from the corporate planning department.

A communication from a member of top management naturally affirms the support and interest necessary for the planning effort. The annual transmittal letter is a common method for restating the significance that is attached to the planning program.

A number of such messages set forth reasons for the long-range planning process, and for the attendant common format and guidelines. Some assurance of flexibility in presenting the unit's plans usually balances the defense of standardization.

Such messages may comment in a general way on the need for planning, the importance of putting forth best efforts, and current serious concerns, such as inflation or the energy shortage, that affect the corporation. Sometimes a key issue selected to highlight the current year's planning, such as product-line analysis or inventory reduction, is emphasized in the letter.

A brief evaluation of the previous year's planning exercise — its successes and failures — is very often a prelude to the announcement of the current year's new emphasis' or focus in the corporate planning exercise. This is followed by a statement of the changes being made in planning procedures, e.g., elimination of some forms, introduction of contingency planning.

Some transmittal letters contain the calendar of the planning cycle or key dates, depending on how explicitly this is treated later on in the guides.

Almost always, there is an invitation to call the corporate planning department — with names and telephone numbers — for clarification or help with problems.

Advice on utilizing the organization's computer, and even brief rundowns on its possibilities, may be outlined. And it is not unusual to find the formulas and methods of arriving at profit figures that are needed for some sections of the plan.

Several companies direct specific advice at past sources of difficulty. For example, division

Exhibit 5: Review Presentation — An Industrial Machinery Manufacturer

The following [is] a set of thirteen standardized visuals that will be required for all presentations. These standardized slides are being requested to insure a consistent review of key sections of the long-range business plan.

The thirteen standardized slides are:

SLIDE 1　　　　Business charter
SLIDE 2　　　　Objectives
SLIDE 3　　　　Market and sales plan
SLIDE 4　　　　Competitive environment

　　　　SLIDE 4a　　　Competitive strategies (Competitor "A")
　　　　SLIDE 4b　　　Competitive strategies (Competitor "B")
　　　　SLIDE 4c　　　Competitive strategies (Competitor "C")

SLIDE 5　　　　Realized price and cost reduction
SLIDE 6　　　　Strategic action programs
SLIDE 7　　　　Operating results
SLIDE 8　　　　Capital utilization
SLIDE 9 ,　　　Division investment
SLIDE 10　　　Profitability trends and projections

The standardized visuals are intended to be used with other visuals developed by the division. They may be interspersed with these other visuals, or used in any order desired by the division general manager in order to present the division's plan most effectively.

Exhibit 6: Review Agenda — A Manufacturer of Industrial Products

	Minutes or Percent of Presentation Time
1. Review of year's financial results to date compared to plan.	5 minutes
2. Progress report on *key* short-term and long-term objectives.	10 minutes or 5 – 10% of time
3. Presentation of fact sheets, product line P&L's, and strategy for each selected product line or business unit.	25 – 35%
4. Discussion and approval of strategies.	25 – 35%
5. Discussion of capital needs.	5 – 10%
6. Review of 1975-1978 numbers developed in September 1973 (updated if you feel necessary).	5 – 10%
7. Develop corporate key issues for each group (to be done by Plan Review Committee during corporate session).	–––

Note: Presentation time may be altered by each group to conform to its own special needs.

managers are frequently reluctant to make written estimates for which they fear they may be held strictly accountable. A manufacturing firm urges the necessity of the "best estimate," even on limited information. "Reporting of these estimates," it suggests, "is not so much for purposes of approval but to provide stimulus for discussions of long-range plans and programs."

A large diversified corporation wants "management's realistic estimate of what is *most likely* to happen — not an optimistic 'sales' goal which is probably unattainable, nor an overly conservative 'safe' forecast, which is useless."

Another company advises its managers to maintain "a balance between accuracy and undue effort" in developing the input for its resource plan. Its recommendations for preparation point out: "The data derived from this section will be used to develop preliminary financial data for future requirements and will not, in and of itself, become a firm capital budget. Consequently, it does not warrant the effort that these items receive in your annual forecast."

One planning manual offers suggestions by divisions that have found ways to ease their planning efforts. Another manual cautions against allowing all levels of the organization to use the manual because "smaller departments or functions will tend to create excessive paperwork or undertake difficult analyses for which they are not properly staffed." A further bit of advice, for the appraisal process in particular, is that consideration may be given to a process of scanning previous years' material for changes rather than undertaking a complete bottom-up redo every year.

Illustrative Devices

A common ploy in getting planners to address key issues is to pose a set of questions for the topic being developed. This may involve only a few key issues, or it may be so detailed that it runs into hundreds of questions for the division executive to find the answers to. Sometimes these questions are built right into the form required for submission.

To illustrate what is wanted for different portions of the plan, examples are often given. (Sometimes explicitly bad examples are given as well, to forestall poor results.) One manual uses a hypothetical "Division Z" to demonstrate every part of the plan requirements. Sample filled-in forms are another popular method of illustrating what is wanted. A pharmaceutical goods manufacturer has found it useful, for communications as well as educational purposes, to distribute a good plan prepared by one division to other divisions in the company.

One of the most comprehensive manuals studied for this report is that of an industrial machinery manufacturer. As an aid in using the manual, color-coded pages are used for each individual section treating every document to be submitted. Each section covers format requirements, instructions for filling out the format, example of a completed format page, and planning concepts relating to the information being displayed.

Definitions

Planning, like many other management functions, tends to acquire a terminology of its own. To compound this problem, there is no widespread agreement on terminology among planners. Yet terms used in planning must be understood by all who participate in the planning process in order to get the results desired.

Even more important than the conflict that jargon can provoke between the planning department and divisions, misinterpretations of seemingly obvious concepts — objective, goal, strategy — can produce frustrations and wasted effort at both the top and bottom levels of the planning exercise. Thus planning terms and concepts are defined in the instructions given to divisions. As one manual explains it, this is to "ensure that all personnel directly or indirectly associated with the planning process are speaking the same language."

One company prefaces its definitions with this statement: "In working with managers throughout the company, we have found that the meanings of management terms tend to vary widely, particularly in the function of planning. These differences in interpretation make communication more difficult.

"This glossary is an attempt to define, clearly and precisely, the meanings of planning terms most commonly used and perhaps most often misunderstood in our practice of management by objectives and results. These terms will serve as the official definitions until formally changed."

One firm that prints a short glossary of its key planning words takes a firm stand on its own definitions: "It is recognized that these terms may be defined in many ways; however, within [the company's] planning process it is essential that we have uniformity of definition."

The definition of planning words and terms is not a simple exercise. The best-thought-out examples often backfire, and what one planner may consider immune to misinterpretation may reveal ambiguities in the very next planning cycle.

In most manuals, definitions of planning terms appear at the beginning of the instructions for a particular section of the plan; in some guides, however, they are treated separately, as glossaries. These range in size from four to five key words to as many as 70 specific definitions of terms used in the instructions. They may bear little resemblance to dictionary definitions, and often are not indicative of common usage.

The most frequently defined terms encountered in 28 lists of definitions in this study are *objective, strategy* (22 times each), and *goal* (14 times). It is even deemed necessary to define *planning* and *plan* (8 and 7 times, respectively).

References

Ongoing educational programs in planning for managers are reflected in several company manuals that contain substantial planning bibliographies. Such source material is usually distributed at planning seminars or orientation programs; including it in the planning manual itself is intended to encourage continuing study of planning concepts and other relevant matters.

This keeps managers abreast of developments that may bear on their planning expertise and their functioning as managers.

A pharmaceutical firm that is putting special emphasis on an analysis of the total business environment for plotting strategy prints a 10-page list of books, articles and reports with its planning guides. These are the sources for a statement of the business environment — kept current and international in scope — issued annually to the managers. It is designed as a catalyst to division heads to look outside their own immediate businesses and product lines, to consider key trends in the future and their impact on the business. The sources cover trends in the health industry, business, social and political fields, as well as the subject of planning.

In one company that holds regular planning seminars for its officers, the planning manual is one of the documents studied. For this purpose it contains seven pages of categorized publications on various aspects of planning. For example, under the subject of "Appraisal," there are four headings: General; The Environment: Social, Economic, Political, Technical; Competitive Information; and Market Information.

The planner for a health products manufacturer reproduces articles from the business literature that he considers particularly timely or pertinent for the managers. It is "a grace note" in the effort at communication, he comments, sometimes read, sometimes not.

The Corporate Self-Image

As further guide to the divisions in making up their plans, some companies issue statements defining their own views of their position in the business community or in society in general. This provides a framework in which the division or subsidiary can position itself vis-à-vis the corporation.

These declarations of the corporate image are found in the planning documents in this study under a variety of titles: Corporate Mission, Purpose, Philosophy, Objectives, or even Strategy. For the most part, they attempt to broadly characterize the business and how the company will conduct itself.

Corporate Mission, Purpose, Policies

The self-scrutiny corporate top managements urge on their divisions and subsidiaries is not always apparent in the planning manuals they issue. Perhaps some corporate charters or missions appear in other documents, and are omitted from the literature issued for the planning effort; in any event, few examples of corporate mission are found in the planning manuals that were submitted for analysis in this study.

One such statement is offered by a publishing company, which defines its purpose as "to create, develop and manufacture products (as well as after-products and by-products), and to offer services which are vehicles for sales and marketing efforts with emphasis on advertising. In every area of market participation, [company] products should attempt to distinguish themselves on the basis of *Service* as opposed to other appeals."

A West Coast bank holding company's stated mission is "to selectively position ourselves in worldwide markets, offering profitable financial and financially related services to meet the changing needs of consumers, businesses, governments and others in those markets."

One company that incorporates its strategy in its planning guide states it as:

"[The company] will remain primarily a manufacturer, emphasizing internal growth, international as well as domestic, and distinctive wood and related products which require innovation, special aesthetic features or fabrication, and significant marketing skills."

Statements of the basic policies of the corporation are spelled out more often than corporate charters. A business forms manufacturer, for example, details in its planning manual basic corporate policies on the following: shareholders, dividends, profit measurement, planning organization, control, marketing, manufacturing, engineering and research, finance, employee relations, purchasing, and mergers and acquisitions.

Corporate Objectives, Goals

The basic corporate objectives or goals that are issued in planning guides are different from the types of objectives required from divisions. They are generally less specific in nature and are usually not quantified. (A number of companies issue objectives and goals separately at the beginning of the planning cycle.)

Corporate objectives and goals are generally couched in philosophical terms and are frequently addressed to the corporation's role as profit maker, business leader, employer and citizen.

Some corporate objectives found in the documents submitted for this study follow.

"1. To continually improve the quality and effectiveness of management through the selection, development and utilization of outstanding people.

2. To encourage, foster and stimulate the development and growth of new products and new markets by divisions.

3. To identify and pursue acquisitions in high-growth markets.

4. To maximize profitability and return on investment under any economic conditions through better utilization of resources, a constant surveillance of operations, and strict financial controls.

5. To recognize changing economic conditions and to redeploy affected assets.

6. To achieve annual productivity improvement in all divisions."

— A diversified industrial products firm

* * *

"A. Support the fact that we are primarily a human institution dedicated to an organizational philosophy which promotes professional excellence and employee initiative.

"B. Recognize that our institution is a citizen of a society and therefore accepts the responsibility to contribute the resolution of external environmental problems — our existence depends on whether our society accepts us as a provider of needed services and whether we contribute to the well-being of our society and economy.

"C. Plan for the maximization of wealth over the long run for the sake of perpetuity — we seek growth and profits, not as ends in themselves but as a means of perpetuating our existence for the well-being of our employees, our society, and our economy. Our goal is to achieve superior performance through an aggressive, balanced growth program, stressing the need for product and service innovation aimed at minimizing our sensitivity to single product line dependency.

"D. Meet the challenge of the continuing need to manage change.

"E. As a service business specializing in financial activity we want to honor the privilege afforded us as a financial institution and to maintain an image of security — an image that says [the bank] is a sound institution which aims to protect stockholder investment and the safety of customer assets and interests."

— A New England bank

*   *   *

"A. To maintain a position of leadership in the business forms field and to attain a position of leadership in the fields of promotional printing, source data collection, and other related peripheral equipment and data services.

"B. To maintain itself in a sound financial condition and to obtain for its shareholders a fair and proper return on their investment, commensurate with the risks inherent in the nature of its business.

"C. To provide its employees with good working conditions; to pay wages and salaries in line with those prevailing in its industry and the local industries in communities in which our plants are located, for similar work requiring like responsibilities, experience and skills; and to provide employment as secure and as steady as is practical, commensurate with the risks in its industry.

"D. To be a good neighbor in the communities in which it is located and to foster and promote safety and health and other civic activities directed toward the fundamental improvement of those communities.

"E. To provide a continuity of management to perpetuate the successful operation of the company.

"F. To strengthen its position in the worldwide markets through the extension of "know-how" agreements and by other means, if sound business judgment and conditions so warrant."

— A business forms manufacturer

*   *   *

An agricultural cooperative, whose goals were developed by its management and approved by its board of directors, states five long-range goals toward which its planning is directed. The goals and rationale for each are stated in these areas: basic farm business, diversification, food marketing, profit and growth. The last is described this way:

"Growth
"Achieve a rate of growth which will optimize the utilization of our facilities and the opportunities for our people.
"Rationale
"a. The organization that does not grow will stagnate.
"b. Growth provides:
— New and better ways to serve members.
— Increased volume to offset rising costs.
— Opportunities for greater profit.
— Greater job security and opportunity, enabling [the organization] to attract and hold good employees."

Part 3:
Instructions for the Division Plan

THE MAIN PURPOSE of corporate planning guides is to help managers develop long-range plans for their divisions. Therefore, instructions for preparing the constituent parts of these plans comprise the bulk of the planning manuals and other guides.

Almost all long-range divisional or subsidiary plans contain the elements described here, but one finds differences in the nomenclature, interrelationships, emphases and sequence of these elements. Further, there is inevitably some overlapping of the elements. The internal analysis of the business, for example, contains some external components – such as the position of company products in relation to competition. In a number of manuals, too, some of the elements are combined, as is evident in several of the exhibits included in the report.

Each element of the divisional plan is treated discretely here in order to give as full discussion as possible. The sequence of presentation reflects the most typical practices found in the documents submitted for this study.

The Executive Summary

The executive summary, frequently asked for in division or subsidiary plans, is a condensed version of the detailed account of the business's financial, strategic and performance outlook over the next few years. It generally serves as the basis of discussion at planning review meetings.

The summary serves as an initial presentation of the plan, after which corporate executives can examine more closely those portions that they wish to probe in detail. Where brevity and conciseness are not important considerations, the executive summary may not be required. Some corporate executives are perfectly willing, even eager, to peruse the sometimes voluminous amount of paper constituting a division's plan.

A bank, which requests a "brief, primarily qualitative summary of the key elements and

ideas" in its departments' plans, gives the purpose of this section as:

"A. Provide top management with an overview of what will be discussed in the detail of your 1975 plans.

"B. Provide the necessary background information to support your 1975 plans.

"C. Serve as a focal point for consolidating, monitoring and updating departmental plans."

Sometimes the executive summary is merely a narrative describing the key aspects of the attached planning documents; in other cases, financial summaries are expected as well (see Exhibits 7-9). These are some typical contents of executive summaries:

". Comparison to previous year's plans.

". Major planning assumptions (produced from a review of internal and external environments and trends).

". Growth strategy and business goals.

". Optimization plan: existing business.

". New business development: goals and major programs.

". Operations: priorities, goals and major programs.

". Organization/management development: priorities, goals and major programs.

". Financial: priorities, goals and major programs.

". Financial summary."

— A food processor

* * *

"Mission, General Strategy, Strategic Action Programs, Operating Action Programs, Critical Actions and Events Summary, Contingency Plans, and Situation Analysis."

— A paper manufacturer

* * *

". . . the introduction and summary should include a description of the environment in

Exhibit 7: Executive Summary Instructions — A Capital Goods, Automotive and Consumer Products Company

The final step in preparing the strategic plan is to develop a narrative which provides an introduction and a summary for the accompanying documents. It should highlight the direction that management plans to give to the division, and outline the philosophy and assumptions used to develop the plan. It should deal with major issues and provide a synopsis and interpretation of information contained in the accompanying documents rather than repeat that information.

The narrative should be concise, to the point and as short as possible. However, it should deal separately with each product line of the division and each of the major operating functions of the division. When the operating functions of marketing, engineering, manufacturing, administration, employee relations, and general management are not covered by specific action programs, a statement of strategic planning considerations relating to each should be given in the narrative. If an "action program" on manpower planning is not included, particular attention should be given in the narrative to highlighting the division's efforts in this area.

The narrative may include some key numerical data taken from the accompanying documents when necessary for clarity and understanding; however, it is not intended that the narrative include extensive numerical data.

The narrative should deal with the main thrust to be given to the overall division and to each product line.

which you expect to operate during the next three years. It also will include a summary of the expectations (growth, investment, return, changes, etc.) and a statement of all the assumptions critical to the achievement of the plan."

— A diversified industrial products company

* * *

"Summary — a recapitulation of significant accomplishments planned during the next five years including (a) a concise statement of your business strategy, (b) a master schedule, and (c) anticipated results expressed in terms of annual sales and earnings capacity.

"a. Strategy — a concise one-page statement of your general business strategy for use by senior management.

"b. Master Schedule — a schedule integrating operational and development programs that sets forth, in tabular form, specific dates against which future progress can be measured. . . .

"c. Performance Estimates — preliminary estimates of future performance expressed in terms of anticipated annual sales and earnings and capital expenditures required during the period."

— A newspaper publisher

* * *

"I. Major Specific Objectives
   a. Summary of financial performance.
   b. Sales and profits for existing product lines.
   c. Sales and profits for new and discontinued product lines.
   d. Capacity/production statistics by plant and product.
"II. Major Programs
"III. Resources Required
"IV. Source and Disposition of Funds
"V. Obstacles
"VI. Priority Addendum"

— A tire manufacturer

In this example, "priority addendum" is a brief written supplement to the plan outlining any additional projects that would be undertaken if more capital were made available. It is not included in the basic plan. It consists of a description of the project; a brief paragraph explaining why the program is essential or desirable; and a simplified flow-of-funds statement showing fixed assets, working funds, sales and profits, by year, for each venture. These are listed in priority with attention to their return on investment.

* * *

(text continued on page 28)

Exhibit 8: Executive Summary Instructions — A Construction Equipment Company

Executive Summary — Overview

The purpose of this section is to summarize the results of the proposed plan. It includes a management summary letter, financial summary, and a brief description of where the division is going and how it expects to get there.

Executive Summary — Instructions

This is a cover letter from the Division President to his Group Vice President. While no specific format is dictated, certain items are suggested below which should probably be covered in the summary. It is intended that this summary should enable the Division President to set the stage for the formal plan in his own words.

- Items which should be incorporated in the executive summary may include:

- Summary of profit and sales goals over the next five years including:

    - Sales
    - Profit Before Tax
    - PBT as percent of Sales
    - Percent ROA

- Significant characteristics of the division:

    - Opportunities
    - Strengths
    - Weaknesses
    - Threats

- Basic strategy of the division

- Brief summary of the development plan

- Brief summary of functional plans

    - Marketing
    - Engineering
    - Manufacturing
    - Purchasing/Material Control
    - M.I.S.
    - Personnel
    - Export
    - Financial

- Complete financial summary (Exhibit A)

- List significant events

The summary letter can be of any length, but two or three pages with appropriate attachments should suffice if the letter is confined to significant points. Please refer to the Planning Guide for specific instructions on the [company's] planning process.

Exhibit 8 (continued)

Exhibit A:
BUSINESS PLAN (1975 - 1979)
FINANCIAL SUMMARY

_____ DIVISION   DATE _____

ACTUAL				(Thousands of Dollars)	Current Estimate	GOALS			
1971	1972	1973	1974		1975	1976	1977	1978	1979
				UNFILLED ORDERS					
				NEW ORDERS					
				SALES					
				Annual Percent Change					
				Percent Change 1974/1979	✕	✕	✕	✕	✕
				PRETAX PROFITS					
				Annual Percent Change					
				Percent Change 1974/1979	✕	✕	✕	✕	✕
				Percent of Sales					
				AVERAGE ASSETS					
				Turnover Rate					
				Return on Assets					
				AVERAGE NET PLANT AND EQUIPMENT					
				Sales Per Dollar					
				EMPLOYEE COUNT (AVERAGE)					
				Sales Per Employee					
				NET INCOME					
				DEPRECIATION					
				CAPITAL EXPENDITURES					

Exhibit 9: Executive Summary Outline — A Bank

I. *External Analysis*
    A. Market analysis
    B. Competitive analysis
    C. Environmental factors

II. *Internal Analysis*
    Summarize strengths and weaknesses in . . .
    A. Products/markets;
    B. Administration/management;
    C. Production and distribution of services; and
    D. Historical and present performance

        1. Versus competition
        2. Versus future needs.

III. *Critical Variables*
    Drawing on external and internal appraisals, what are the few critical factors which can "make or break" your longer-run performance, and which of these do you have some element of control over?

    A. What appear to be your best opportunities for profit improvement? Market opportunities? Internal operations?

    B. What are your biggest threats to competitive survival? Competition? Operating costs? Changing markets?

    C. What recognized strengths can you employ? What recognized weaknesses can you shore up?

    D. What are the least attractive services which you now perform and which are using up scarce manpower and capital resources? Can you redeploy in better markets?

IV. *Long-run Objectives and Strategies*
    A. From your analysis of your environment, together with the corporate objectives and strategy guidelines provided, what are the *long-run end results* you believe you must achieve in order to perform successfully and to contribute to successful corporate performance?

    B. For each objective, list the specific *action strategies* you plan to pursue in order to achieve that objective.

"This section should provide a brief historical biography of the business area where pertinent, and a brief statement regarding the future direction and objective that is recommended for the business area (such as expansion, continuing at present level, planned phase-out or divestment, etc.). The section should contain a brief statement regarding the key elements of strategy (such as new product development, application of additional capital and other resources, increased production and facilities, etc.). It should contain a brief statement of key issues and risks that can influence the successful achievement of the strategy. It should contain a brief statement relative to priorities and to the expected payoff if the strategy (or strategies) is undertaken. And it should contain a brief statement to help validate the essential reasons why this . . . direction and strategy is the correct one to follow. Where pertinent, quantitative information should be included."

— An automotive parts manufacturer

Although the summary is the first part of the submitted plan, it is usually the last one written, "the final step in preparing the strategic plan." Recommendations for preparing the summary are offered by a diversified concern:

"Since this is a summary of the overall document, it probably will be most beneficial to prepare this portion after goals, strategies and tactical actions have been defined and the results expected have been determined.

"By keeping notes concerning each critical factor influencing the plan's outcome, as it is developed, the proper material to prepare this section should be available."

Even summaries can run amok in length. An executive of a large automotive concern admits that the summaries ran to 100 pages before the planning system was revised. For this reason, size constraints are often suggested – or demanded – in the instructions for this part of the plan.

A food products manufacturer gives this advice: "The executive summary should consist of three to five pages of narrative and supporting attachments, as required. This can be accomplished by condensing each section of the planning book to one paragraph in the executive summary and including pertinent exhibits (attachments) which are 'lifted' in original form from the planning data in the various sections. Reference to the exhibits can be made in parentheses following the appropriate paragraph."

And a paper manufacturer's manual has this instruction: "The length of the entire text . . . need ordinarily not exceed 25 pages. Free use of charts, diagrams and tables of the unit's own invention to shorten the text and aid in interpretation is recommended."

Statement of Mission, Charter

The division's statement of mission, or charter, usually defines the purpose of the unit, and the limits within which it may operate. It is a fairly stable characterization which, once

An industrial machinery company appends an unusual comment to its discussion of the business charter:

"The business charter encompasses an environment which is much broader than that currently being served. A division should include those functions, markets and customers which are *not* served and those products which are *not* produced. These less familiar aspects defined in the business charter often offer the greatest opportunities for, or threats to, the future success of the division. Thus, each division must be completely frank in appraising those changing aspects of its chartered business which could have an important impact on the division's future success."

written by the division and approved by headquarters, is generally carried over from year to year. Unit charters or revisions to them are generally negotiated with a high management level to ensure that no charter conflicts exist in the organization.

The principal features of the mission or charter are a broad definition of the basic business and scope of the unit. The charter, many manuals advise, should allow for growth of the unit and for potential changes in the environment, in addition to showing current areas of business activity and related areas where the division may expand its scope.

A concern frequently expressed is that a balance must be struck between too wide and

Exhibit 10: Example of a Charter — A Subsidiary of a Food Products Company

The Mail Order Sales Company is a wholly owned subsidiary of [the company] which is organized to market specialty foods, cookware and related products in the United States and Canada under the ["_____"] or manufacturers' brands. Sales are made on a cash basis directly to consumers through direct mail, magazines and product inserts, and also through independent distributors to better quality gift shops. Products are manufactured for the company by [company's] _____ Co., _____ Co., and independent manufacturers under long-term contracts. The company maintains offices and operates out of a 150,000 sq. ft. warehouse and distribution center. The company has been authorized to explore in-home direct sales and better quality cosmetics products as two areas for possible diversification.

Exhibit 11: Example of a Charter — A Division of a Financial Services Firm

> ABC Company will market investment advisory services to any organization requiring investment management advice on their funds (e.g., pension, retirement, etc.) for short or long periods of time. The size of funds to be managed should be over $5 million. The services will be sold by the ABC Company direct to top managements of corporations, unions, private institutions, governments, and on occasion to individual clients with requirements for large money management. The services will be marketed to all 50 states. ABC Company, initially, will buy its investment research services from the outside until it can develop an inside economic research capability.

too narrow a definition. The former could leave a division with no real direction for strategic planning, while too narrow a statement could, in one manual's terminology, "blind us to environmental changes, opportunities and threats." A financial services firm asks its units to write charters that are "broad enough to allow for flexibility and imaginative management yet confined to areas to which the manager is willing to commit resources."

A charter is an "authorization" — a negotiable agreement between the executive office and a general manager — according to a food processor. As such, "since both parties know that the charter is always negotiable, limits can be current and specific and yet not preclude undiscovered or unidentified opportunities."

Besides defining the business and its limits, the mission statements may also include objectives, strategic thrust, policies and guidelines. A paper company asks for "the longest-term objectives of the unit . . . ordinarily [to] be realized beyond a five-year horizon."

The mission of the unit is commonly asked for in terms of market segments, product or service categories, and geographical or other dimensions. One company also wants "the basic needs which give rise to this business" to be identified, as well as the functions performed to fill these needs.

Another company requests in its mission section "major nonrevenue-related values" to be pursued by the unit. These may include such items as style of management, development of morale, equal employment opportunities, training and retraining of employees, and community relations.

The generally unchanging nature of the mission statement is challenged by a bank which regards the definition as a reflection of the manager's own vision and desire for growth. It believes, therefore, "it is forseeable that this definition could itself be subject to continual change."

The Appraisal/Situation Analysis

To get where you want to go — or even find out where you want to go — you have to know where you are. And, sometimes, how you got there to begin with. This is the basic premise upon which the situation analysis called for in all planning exercises is structured. It is one of the most time-consuming, people-involving aspects of the planning process.

The purpose of such an appraisal is, in the words of a rubber products company, "to provide significant information about the current and possible future situations to those who must review, evaluate or approve the plans." A publishing firm lists four functions of this analysis:

"1. To present a comprehensive picture of the profit center's history and current situation.

"2. To know and understand the competitive environment as well as the profit center's own operation.

"3. To build a stepping-stone for other elements of the plan . . . objectives, strategies, etc.

"4. To gain an understanding in depth of all environmental factors affecting the profit center."

A paper company regards the situation analysis as a means of identifying strategic issues relevant to the fulfillment of a business's mission. It also claims that the analysis will uncover issues that are "serious in their current or potential impact on the business unit, but that are not strategic in the sense of involving directional changes for the business or major resource commitments." Addressing these "operating issues," it advises, will result in an operating action program.

Finding out where the business unit is requires a hard look at the environment, both within and without the organization, and an intelligent appraisal of the unit's own condition and possibilities. The proper analysis and application of this information is the foundation upon which objectives and strategies are built. "The reverse process of finding facts to support a plan," states one planning document, "leads to obvious hazards."

This analysis usually covers an assessment of those facets of the external environment that may affect the business, including an analysis of the market and the competition, and an appraisal of internal strengths and weaknesses, and opportunities and threats. Under this broad umbrella may also be gathered economic assumptions, product-line analysis, sociopolitical trends, technological forecasts, cost-price factors, and other data of special concern to a particular company or industry. Evaluation of previous business plans or strategies is another common feature of this part of the plan.

The appraisal process involves the selection and organization of pertinent data culled from enormous amounts of information. It also demands forecasts — often based on uncertainty and judgmental decisions of the environment.

The manner in which various companies go about instructing their managers on gathering and presenting this portion of the plan ranges from a paragraph of offhand suggestions, to tens of pages of reminders and prods of all factors to be considered, to hundreds of questions covering external and internal conditions. Many instructions include forms devised for this purpose.

The remaining pages of this section show how different organizations attempt to elicit the analytical thinking and the kinds of information they want from their divisional managers. Most work on the assumption that the person who is dealing in a particular environment on a day-to-day basis is the one best qualified to assess it. Not all companies require all the analyses shown, and several combine some elements of the appraisal in their instructions.

Corporate Environmental Assumptions, Guidelines

A number of planning documents in this study contain environmental assumptions issued by corporate headquarters for the guidance of their units' planning. Almost invariably, however, they are accompanied by disclaimers, caveats, permission to differ, or requests to supplement or use only relevant parts.

The issuance of assumptions at the start of the planning cycle is predicated on the need for a somewhat uniform base of background data for corporate planning.[1] "The use of common, explicitly stated assumptions fosters consistency in the development of division, group and corporate plans," declares the manual of one industrial machinery manufacturer. It refers to "those specific quantitive and qualitative judgments regarding the future which form the basic premise upon which the plan is structured."

The sets of assumptions range in sophistication from simple inflation projections to worldwide business environment forecasts, replete with industry implications and computer printouts. Many are the output of well-known consulting services. But in some firms in-house environmental forecasts are developed by the planning department itself, the marketing research department, the corporate economist, or other staff.

The most popular assumptions issued are, of course, economic assumptions. They may be general in nature — covering GNP, business and industry trends, wages, prices, etc. — or range a bit further into energy matters, federal fiscal and

[1]See James K. Brown and Rochelle O'Connor, *Planning and the Corporate Planning Director*, Report 627, The Conference Board, 1974, p. 30.

Exhibit 12: Situation Analysis Outline — A Tire and Rubber Producer

1. KEY SUCCESS FACTORS:
   Secrets of success; break-even charts

2. MARKET CHARACTERISTICS:
   Segments; growth trends; customer identification; consumer attitudes; buying habits; geography; pricing

3. COMPETITIVE PROFILES:
   Identification; market shares; typical responses; specific comparisons

4. PRODUCT AND MARKET COMPARISONS:
   Products; promotion; distribution

5. MANUFACTURING FACTORS:
   Process descriptions; inputs; capacity; competitive comparisons; other uses; planning and control systems

6. TECHNOLOGICAL FACTORS:
   Materials; processes; products; customers and other

7. ECONOMIC, SOCIAL, POLITICAL, GOVERNMENTAL FACTORS:
   Economic and demographic forecasts; likely effects of social and political changes; governmental expenditures and purchasing decisions; legislated controls and restrictions

8. INTERNAL ASSUMPTIONS

9. PLANNING GAPS NOW FORESEEABLE:
   Life cycle analysis; size of sales, profits, assets gap; rationale of acquisitions versus internal development; divestment possibilities

10. SWOPT ITEMS:
    Strengths; Weaknesses; Opportunites; Problems; Threats

monetary policy, and regulatory and legislative actions with economic implications. Depending on the particular industry, more specific types of trends may be noted.

International economic factors are discussed in multinational company assumptions; population trends in an insurance company's assumptions; technical developments to the year 1985 are part of a pharmaceutical company's forecast. Financial institutions have specialized interests to consider. (One bank-holding company gives, in addition to a national outlook, a regional outlook for its particular area.)

An economic overview issued by a food processing company offers both forecasts and implications for a wide-ranging field of topics deemed of concern to its managers in their planning. It covers: general economic outlook, financial markets, consumer markets, labor markets, agricultural commodity markets, energy and other resources, transportation, retail food trade, food service, international markets, government regulations, technology, demographics, and changing values and life-styles.

Lest the latter be viewed as a frivolous fling into sociological theorizing, the top planning executive at a publishing and printing concern has stated that "it would appear increasingly that our businesses have a lesser responsiveness to GNP and a greater sensitivity to the consumer's state of mind or life-style. It is probably the most necessary — and at the same time — the weakest link in strategic planning."

Nevertheless, the use of a set of standardized assumptions has often proven neither prudent nor practical for all the units of the same organization. The units themselves may find that the corporate assumptions issued are at variance with their own — and can substantiate their differences. Geographic location, regional or product considerations can all cause variances. Or a division or subsidiary may have a unique set of circumstances from that foreseen by the headquarters planner.

Such situations explain in part why so many manuals allow — if they do not actually encourage — individual units to modify or tailor to their own needs the assumptions necessary to develop their own long-term plans. Indeed, most corporate planning instructions require the divisional development of a set of environmental assumptions as well, and issue detailed advice on achieving it (see page 39).

Another reason for allowing corporate assumptions to be viewed as not quite "cast in

(text continued on page 38)

Exhibit 13: The Appraisal — A Construction Equipment Company

BUSINESS PLAN (1975 — 1979)

SECTION II

Appraisal — Overview

The selection and organization of information and analyses, in a form that is useful for planning, is the purpose of this section. This includes economic, environment and performance assumptions as well as other factors affecting business, including government regulations. Market analysis and [company] penetration for each business segment are also included.

Appraisal — Instructions

The appraisal is comprised of the following five sections:

I. *Environment* — This should include a brief description of external and internal environment factors and assumptions which underlie division sales and profit forecasts. Concise statements giving the assumption and outlining the resulting action are recommended as shown in Exhibit A. Divisions should not limit their assumptions to the list provided but add or substitute appropriate items. The major purpose of the assumptions list is to set the stage or present the environment in which division management feels it will be operating during the subsequent five years. Specific forecasts of division economic assumptions should be shown on Exhibit B. Business Planning will publish a series of five-year forecasts which can be used as guidelines in developing forecasts relating to your specific situations.

EXHIBIT A

_____ DIVISION   DATE _____

BUSINESS PLAN (1975 — 1979)

MAJOR ASSUMPTIONS OF DIVISION BUSINESS

AREA/ITEM	ASSUMPTION	ACTION
1. ECONOMIC	No-growth economy in 1974 with gentle recovery thereafter peaking in 1976.	• Improve margins through cost-reduction programs. • Expand sales through increased market penetration.
2. INFLATION		
3. MARKET ENVIRONMENT		
4. COMPETITIVE ENVIRONMENT		
5. GOVERNMENT LEGISLATION		
6. OTHER EXTERNAL-ENERGY, ETC.		
7. INTERNAL		
8. OTHER		

Exhibit 13 (continued)

EXHIBIT B

_____ DIVISION   DATE _____

BUSINESS PLAN (1975 — 1979)

ECONOMIC ASSUMPTIONS

	PERCENT CHANGE 1969/1974	1975	1976	1977	1978	1979	PERCENT CHANGE 1974/1979
ECONOMY — GENERAL INDICATORS							
A. GROSS NATIONAL PRODUCT							
B. FRB INDEX OF INDUSTRIAL PRODUCTION							
C.							
ECONOMIC ASSUMPTION — RELATED TO DIVISION/GROUP ACTIVITY							
A. INTERCITY TRUCK TONNAGE—TRUCK							
B. NET FARM INCOME — FARM							
C.							
D.							
E.							
F.							

II. _Markets_ — The initial step in analyzing the markets in which the division competes is to subdivide the business into meaningful segments. Market segments group potential customers according to the similarity of their needs, geographic location, and behavioral response to marketing strategy. In each market segment, it is necessary to obtain a measure of the current and potential markets in units and/or dollars and estimates of the market growth rate. This information for the division, the industry and the resulting market share will be supplied on Exhibit C. Some of the questions and factors which might be considered in developing market segment analyses and in writing the text directed to Exhibit C are listed below:

A. _Market Segment Analysis_

1. At what rate has the market been growing?

2. Historically, what are the external market indicators and how do they behave?

3. If industry volume is cyclical, will recovery cause volume to pick up faster than GNP? How cyclical is the industry in relation to GNP?

4. What external environmental factors might cause the industry to grow faster or slower than GNP? Foreign competition? Competition from other industries? Government regulations and pressures?

5. Are industry growth rates during the plan years consistent with historical trends? If not, why?

Exhibit 13 (continued)

EXHIBIT C

_____ DIVISION   DATE _____

BUSINESS PLAN (1975 — 1979)

MARKET ANALYSIS AND [COMPANY] PENETRATION

TOTAL DIVISION MARKET	1974	1975	1976 1977 1978 1979	PERCENT CHANGE 1974/1979
1. UNIT SALES (BY PRODUCT GROUP) A. B. C. D.				
2. INDUSTRY UNIT SALES A. B. C. D.				
3. MARKET SHARE A. B. C. D.				

B. _Market Penetration Analysis_

1.   Identify and discuss customers.

2.   What are customer needs; e.g., service requirements, financing, distribution requirements, etc.?

3.   Is the product price sensitive or can brand loyalty be established? What is the impact for [the company's] share?

4.   Explain the competitive factors that account for the current trend of [the company's] share, irrespective of whether the trend is up or down.

Exhibit 13 (continued)

    C. *Impact of Market and Penetration Analyses on Division Long-Range Goals*

        1. Briefly define the division's planned penetration objectives.

        2. Discuss the critical "stumbling blocks" that are preventing goal achievement. Examples might include poor distribution systems, insufficient advertising, too little emphasis on product development, poor product positioning, not enough management depth, etc.

        3. Indicate steps the division will take to increase [company's] market penetration; e.g., more selling effort, strengthen distribution system, provide better service or more customer financing, etc.

        4. Relate steps that should be taken to achieve plan goals relating to customer needs. Why will steps we are taking to improve penetration satisfy customer needs better than competition?

        5. Evaluate competitive reaction to [company's] moves to increase penetration.

        6. Are we doing enough to react to moves by competition?

III. *Competition* — This section should include an analysis of the following factors:

    A. *Competitive Product Lines* — Information should be displayed as shown in Exhibit D.

    B. *Competitive Strengths and Weaknesses* — Analyze competition versus [company] in these areas:

        1. Market share — current and projected

        2. Price position.

        3. Product strengths.

        4. Distribution systems

        5. Customer image.

        6. Sales and income over last 5 years.

    C. Evaluate competition in major international markets with specific reference to *U.S. sourced* and *foreign sourced* in at least the following areas:

        1. Market share.

        2. Relative pricing versus [company].

        3. Future marketing planning and product planning assumptions.

    D. *Competitive Strategies* — Briefly outline price and product strategies of each major competitor.

IV. *Division Strengths, Weaknesses, Opportunities, Threats* — Evaluate current status of strengths and weaknesses of the division relative to advantageous or disadvantageous *internal* situations within the division. In a similar manner, evaluate advantageous or disadvantageous situations of the division relative to *external* actions by a competitor or in the environment.

V. *Analysis of Previous Strategies* — Lastly, in the appraisal section, evaluate the impact of subsequent events on previous strategies. Indicate changes in current strategy to reflect these identified changes in the business environment.

Exhibit 13 (continued)

EXHIBIT D

DIESEL ENGINES AVAILABLE FROM MAJOR SUPPLIERS (INDUSTRIAL)

(50 – 200 HP)

MANUFACTURER INTERMITTENT BHP	COMPETITORS											
	A	B	C	D	E	F	G	H	I	J	K	L
50	▓	▓					▓	▓				
60	▓	▓							▓		▓	▓
70	▓		▓			▓	▓	▓		▓	▓	
80		▓	▓				▓					▓
90			▓			▓			▓			
100	▓		▓		▓		▓	▓		▓	▓	
110	▓		▓				▓					
120	▓	▓	▓	▓		▓	▓	▓	▓			
130		▓							▓			
140						▓		▓	▓	▓		
150	▓		▓		▓			▓			▓	
160	▓			▓					▓			
170					▓	▓				▓		
180		▓			▓			▓				
190			▓	▓		▓		▓		▓	▓	
200			▓			▓			▓			

ANNUAL SALES

VOLUME

concrete" is that such rigidity would relieve the managers of a great deal of thinking they should do. From interviews with planners participating in this study, many consider a careful analysis of a unit's distinctive environmental situation an integral element of successful planning. Accepting a ready-made forecast unthinkingly is not conducive to creative effort or original strategy.

Thus one finds a number of statements accompanying corporate environmental analyses that permit planning managers to disagree with or modify such assumptions. Here is how some of them are worded:

"It remains the responsibility of each individual division and group to use only those assumptions which most truly reflect the future as seen by that division or group . . . Assumptions . . . should be changed or added to as each organization sees fit, provided . . . the plan explicitly states the change made . . . and group executive approval obtained."

* * *

"Projections of wage, price and other pertinent company and industry trends should be tailored to the unit's unique environment."

* * *

"If you disagree with the economic trends projected by the (company economic council), be prepared to advise me of your differences and their significance to your long-range plans when we meet in August."

Perhaps the statement of one diversified firm exemplifies the permissive attitude that exists in many firms toward the assumptions they issue:

"We will also attempt to periodically keep you appraised of the economic climate in general . . . the specific trends that may affect your industry in order that you may take this into consideration when developing or modifying your plans."

Financial Guidelines

Regardless of the amount of discretion accorded units on the environmental assumptions prepared for them by corporate headquarters, the financial guidelines — or assumptions — emanating from headquarters are usually of a much more binding nature.[2]

All units of an organization are generally required to key their plans to common corporate percentage or numerical guidelines in critical financial areas in order to properly coordinate the total corporate plan. Obviously, if all units adopted their own financial assumptions, comparisons — and, therefore, consolidation — would be very much out of joint.

An industrial machinery company, that provides planning assumptions for its groups and divisions on business conditions; salaries, wages and fringe benefits; and material and transportation prices, permits the units to change or add to these assumptions, but adopts a completely different stance on its financial

---

[2] *Guideline*, as used here, means data given to be used as a standard, even though it may be referred to as an *assumption* in the planning document.

guidelines. These are mandatory as stated. They cover the capital charge rate, the corporate charge rate, and the assumed income tax rate.

A publisher issues financial guidelines to be followed in its units' five-year forecast on: interest rates, inflation factor, income tax rates, investment tax credit, and dividends to the parent company.

Another firm gives these instructions: "All dollar figures used in the 1975-1979 long-term plan are to be in 1975 Operating Plan dollars, held constant for all forecasts and projections used in the plan years 1976 through 1979. This is advisable for the purpose of uniformity and consolidation of figures.

"Specifically, when forecasting for the base year, 1975 (Operating Plan), use costs and prices as of January 1, 1975 plus planned increases during 1975 coming from a known (expected) rise in the cost of labor, materials, etc., and which will, in turn, result in a price increase. As before, there is to be no separate factoring-up for inflation."

An updated set of inflation assumptions for commodity prices, wages and salaries, interest rates, construction and land costs, and services, fees and billed expenses is issued each year by a food processor for its businesses' financial projections "to insure that all plans are submitted on a comparable basis."

Divisional Environmental Assumptions

Although many companies furnish their divisions with economic and other environmental assumptions, most expect each unit to develop a set of assumptions relevant to its business. A diversified firm expresses it this way.

"As the individual who is most knowledgeable about specific divisional activities and industry trends, you are best able to assess available information, make preliminary judgments as to relevance, and ultimately develop a listing of the most pertinent social, political, technological, economic and competitive conditions likely to underlie future operations."

To explain the necessity for divisional assumptions to its managers, a farm machinery manufacturer introduces this portion of the plan requirements this way:

"The rapid rate of change in our total environment makes it increasingly difficult to predict the future with accuracy because it won't be like the past . . . or as we think it's going to be. The only thing we can say with certainty is that the rate of change will be faster tomorrow than it was yesterday. . . . To further compound the problem, our increasing lead time requirements make it imperative that we have a way to estimate those future developments which will have a substantial

Financial Schedules

For the financial data required by the corporate level, imaginations are not fired. No matter that some portions of the plan challenge creativity and originality, financial schedules are always standard and traditional. This facilitates consolidation and assures consistency, even though the accounting procedures may produce more data than is really necessary for the plan.

The amount and detail of the financial information may vary from company to company — some are much more financially oriented than others — but almost always include summaries of capital expenditures, balance sheet, income statements, and cash flow. Other financial information that may also be requested includes: profitability assessment, sales and contributions, source and use of funds, return on net assets employed, tax schedules, debt schedules, and so on.

Invariably these figures are analyzed in their historical context, and show both historical and forecast data for a fixed number of previous and future years, plus current year.

impact on our business, function or strategic programs.

"In general, assumptions can be divided into two categories — broad assumptions about the world in which you live and assumptions specifically concerned with your business or function. The first category might include managerial, sociopolitical, economic and technological assumptions. Assumptions applying directly to your activity could include the future nature of your business or function, future environment and future capabilities. . . .

"In a complex, rapidly changing, unpredictable environment, it is impossible to plan without the use of assumptions. You cannot predict the future with accuracy . . . but you cannot plan for the future unless you create an estimate of what you think is going to happen . . . and your management team cannot plan together unless you all share the same estimate. That is why 'assumptions' are so

essential — and the most important ones should be quantified so it is easier to identify, detect and measure deviations."

Assumptions, according to a bank participating in this study, "are an important trigger device for planning. When in the process of carrying out your plans an explicit assumption changes or is violated, you are automatically reminded to check thoroughly that planned actions are still correct. Therefore, assumptions perform an important service throughout the duration of a plan and not just in its developmental phase."

These are some ways in which companies ask for this section of the plan.

"Environmental Assessment — What are the opportunities and threats of your business as they relate to the present environmental dimensions and to your prediction of their future scope?

"A. Political and international policies
    1. National and international policies.
    2. Traditional government regulations.
    3. Political and social developments.
    4. Economic developments.

"B. Market dimensions
    1. Changes in market or product demand.
    2. Changes in market requirements.
    3. Changes in distribution requirements.

"C. Product and technological dimensions
    1. Changes in products and services being offered.
    2. Innovative changes in processes and technological development required to produce products.
    3. Changes in raw material or ingredients.
    4. Other.

"D. Competitive dimensions
    1. Major competition and their changing character.
    2. Comparison of your business with that of the competition."

        — A container manufacturer
          *   *   *

Exhibit 14: Commentary on Environmental Assumptions — A Paper Company

The development of the business plan will require the establishment of a set of assumptions by the unit. Documentation of the major assumptions made is critical to the usefulness and tractability of the plan. In general, these assumptions will fall into one of three categories:

1. Those related to the outcome of uncertain events as they impact on the implementation of specific strategic and operating action programs. These assumptions should be listed within those sections of the Executive Summary.

2. Those related to uncertain environmental conditions that impact on the business unit's performance, but that are not the subject of an action program. For example, economic indicators, governmental actions, technological developments, etc. These assumptions should be documented in the Situation Analysis.

3. Those used to transform the plan into definitive financial projections. For example, price increases, raw material cost inflation, labor cost inflation, productivity increases, employment levels, working capital rates, etc. These assumptions *must* be documented in the Situation Analysis. The following tabular format is recommended and, at minimum, the indicated items should be stated:

	1974	1975	1976	1977	1978	1979
Price Change (%)	6.2	. . . .				
Raw Material Cost Inflation (%)	7.4	. . . .				
Manpower Cost Inflation (%)	6.1	. . . .				
Productivity Increase (%)	2.0	. . . .				
. . .						
Hourly Employees	840	. . . .				
Exempt Employees	110	. . . .				
Non-Exempt Employees	38	. . . .				
Total Employees	988	. . . .				
. . .						
Inventory/Net Sales ($)	.165	. . . .				
Receivables/Net Sales ($)	.061	. . . .				
Other Net W.C./Net Sales ($)	(.035)	. . . .				
Net W.C./Net Sales	.191	. . . .				
. . .						

"Assumptions should be presented in two areas. First, a statement should be made regarding the expected availability of critical resources such as management, products capacity, availability of locations, raw materials, etc. Second, the division should list external factors which may have a plus or minus 5 percent effect on profits in any one of the next three years. These areas might include product technology, competition, customer relationships, etc. [Examples]

"Some explanation and justification for all assumptions should be included as part of this schedule."

— A consumer products company
* * *

"Analysis should be made of all important aspects of the division's business environment, with particular emphasis on those that have changed significantly in the past year or so. This area can probably be developed most conveniently by considering the following categories: Political factors and the legal climate; markets, including growth rates, regulatory aspects, pricing; developments in transportation; socioeconomic factors; technological developments; competition; customers; consumers."

— A grain company
* * *

"Industry characteristics and trends. Cover basic economic forces affecting the industry: fragmentation, consolidation trends, growth rates, price trends, trade practices, changes in method of distribution.

"Planning assumptions. Key assumptions about external factors which have an important influence on the unit's business but over which [the company] has no control, such as GNP, market growth rates, population trends, government controls, social developments, fashion trends, price and cost trends, raw material supply, etc."

— A diversified firm
* * *

"Industry Profile — Updated: An updated statement of the assumptions made about the industry in which the profit center operates. This statement should include commentary in the following areas:

"A. Economic Factors: Changes in general economy or specific subsegments affecting the profit center.

"B. Consumer profile and behavior: Changes in purchase behavior, life-styles, mobilities, spending levels, etc.

"C. Market consumption trends: Changes by region, user characteristics, store types, etc.

"D. Competition: Trends in market share, type, numbers, location, intensity, aggressiveness; changes in pricing, promotion, products, packaging, media plan, advertising copy, etc.

"E. Distribution and trade: Changes in buying practices, distribution practices and channels, warehousing, delivery services, storage, freight rates, etc.

"F. Government regulations: Laws, industry and consumer pressures, energy and environmental legislation, etc.

"G. Technological changes: Any changing technology affecting the business environment of the profit center.

"H. Industry financial ratios: Industry averages versus profit center:
Percent Net Profit/Sales
Percent Return on Equity
Percent Long Term Debt/Total Capital
Capital Turnover."

— A food processor
* * *

"Environmental Assumptions Needed for Preparation of the Corporate Plan

"1. Sales forecasts on cash flow basis
"2. Product redemptions and terminations
"3. Underwriting and commission rates (1973-1977)
"4. Funds management (1973-1977)
"5. Interest rates on borrowed money
"6. New investment yields
"7. Personnel
"8. Other expense
"9. Federal and state taxes
"10. General indicators."

— A financial services firm
* * *

"Prepare a numbered list of 'Assumptions' (factors key to your division achieving its objectives, but over which you have no control), e.g., raw material and labor costs . . . market or demand levels, government action, industry prices, etc. Use specific rates where applicable. Also, list any specific division price increases planned. . . ."

— A hardboard processor

* * *

"The External Environmental Appraisal section of the preliminary plans should be a summary of trends in three areas:

"I. Broad socioeconomic trends personalized to the specific parameters of the division.

"II. Competitive conditions in the industry (size, growth, outlook, key competitors, channels of distribution), and [the company's] position vis-à-vis the most important competitors.

"III. Consumer and market trends in the industry and [the company's] positioning vis-à-vis principal customer groups.

"In writing environmental assessments, general managers should keep in mind the following caveats:

". We are looking for summaries of trends and not detailed expositions on them.
". It is natural to concentrate on the next year or two but we hope to begin to extend our horizons a full five years or more. For example, if it takes more than five years to project a product or industry life cycle, we hope divisions will look beyond fiscal year 1979.
". We hope environmental assessments will be thorough, but, at the same time, they should concentrate on significant trends and not attempt to encompass every possible contingency.
". Environmental assessments are not intended to stand on their own. They should be related to specific business decisions and to

other sections of the plan — i.e., the charter, objectives and strategies."

— A food products manufacturer

* * *

"The environmental assumptions include those changes of a social, political, economic and technical nature which are expected to have an impact on the business of the planning unit. Since the total environment is extensive, the selection of factors to consider should be based upon a determination of the sensitivity of the business to each factor. The probability of occurrence of a change should also influence the selection, but it is well to include certain low-probability occurrences that may have a major impact, since they are properly the subject of contingency plans."

— An instrument and machinery firm

External Analysis: The Market, the Competition

The key elements of the situation analysis are the market and the competition. Some companies, in fact, do not even require any examination of the broader environment, or even an appraisal of the unit's internal condition. A thorough analysis of market factors and competitive factors furnishes a large part of the answer to "Where are we now?"

But unless it is willing to be inundated with raw and undigested information, the corporate level must lay down some guidelines for the form in which it wishes to receive market and competitor data. Perhaps for this reason, more forms and instructions appear among the planning documents for this section of the planning procedure than for any other. Getting the division, subsidiary or other unit to develop a comprehensive fact base from which to select and present those elements critical to the plan preoccupies many corporate planning departments.

"If all the questions of the situation analysis were considered and carefully answered, the resulting number of pages might run into the hundreds," states one planning manual that lists a number of such questions as an aid in developing a fact base for the plan. "Yet these must be summarized into only a few pages. The time, effort and expense of obtaining this information must also be considered," it goes on. "Perhaps each year current and accurate answers to a select group of questions can be sought. In this way, over a period of three or four years, most of the important questions will have been answered."

Data concerning the market are examined from many angles: market segment, demand, requirements, share, growth rate, size, customer, innovation, prices; breakdowns of international, domestic and regional statistics; and the division's own product-line analysis.[3]

Competitor information can rival company market data in the complexity of the analysis and volume of paper produced. Market position, share, strengths and weaknesses, strategies, objectives, profits and products can be probed for each competitor identified. And since much of this information is not easily available, the amount of time and research involved can be ominous.

Corporate guidance for analyzing the market and competition takes many forms. On the whole, the long-range plan is supposed to reflect the synthesis of the data collected, and most guides do not go into detail on the gathering of this information. Presumably this routine is in the marketing department's domain.

The excerpts which follow show how different companies request these data.

"The primary areas to be investigated for this section are the market and the competition. However, the implication on pro-

ducts, technology, resources and financial parameters are readily apparent. Examples of several factors to be included in the analysis and discussion are summarized below. It is intended that these examples cover all types of market, including aftermarkets, service, R and D, etc.

1. *Business Area Market Factors*

a. *Market segment* — i.e., a definition of the particular segment of the market in which the business area is (or is proposing to be) involved. A business area may have more than one market segment.

b. *The size and growth trend of the market segment* — This should be a *quantitative* description of the information where possible.

c. *The type and size of customer* the business area would interface with in the market segment. Both *quantitative and qualitative* descriptions of the information should be given where possible.

d. *Market innovation trends* to which the business area must respond or be aware of. This will be a qualitative statement of the information.

e. *Normal product life cycle* — i.e., a statement of the number of years that a product in this business area would be in production and sold in the market.

f. *Deficiencies and/or requirements of the market* — This represents an identification statement of an existing market demand where a deficiency exists in current product approaches or where a new requirement exists for either an existing product or a new product.

g. *International opportunity* — This represents an identification of where and what kind of international opportunity does or might exist for a business area. Here it will be necessary for domestic operations to consult with [the international unit] and [the international unit] to consult with the appropriate domestic operation.

h. *Technological trends* — This represents an identification of technology trends in a

[3] See also the following Conference Board Reports: David S. Hopkins, *The Short-Term Marketing Plan*, Report 565, 1972; Stanley J. PoKempner and Earl L. Bailey, "Sales Forecasting Practices," *Experiences in Marketing Management* 25, 1970; "Sales Analysis," *Studies in Business Practices* 113, 1965; "Forecasting Sales," *Studies in Business Practices* 106, 1963 (under revision).

business area to define the timing and type of new technology that can or will be introduced to either obsolete existing products or gain a competitive advantage with a new product for the same application.

i. *System and product integration trend* — This represents an identification of areas in which current products and/or systems face the possibility (or threat) of being integrated with other products or systems to form a new approach to the market. The nature of the integration should also be identified.

j. *Alternative approaches and products* — This represents an identification of the alternatives available to participate in a particular market segment including both hardware and software approaches.

k. *Major factors affecting success or failure* — This represents an identification of the several critical areas that affect success or failure in the market segment, such as product design, price, selection of distributors, volume production, etc.

l. *Key issues* — This represents a summary identification of those identifiable issues which will either enhance or depress the opportunity for success in the market segment. For example, government legislative action on antiskid braking at a particular date, or achieving a specific sales volume at a particular date, may be key issues related to participation in the market segment.

2. Business Area Competitive Factors

The following examples apply to each business area. If a business area has more than one product, an analysis may be required for each product.

a. Competing companies including [the company] — This represents a listing of the companies who participate (or might participate in the case of a new area) in the market segment (or segments) in the business area being analyzed.

b. Competitor sales level and trend — This is for each of the competitors listed in (a) above including [the company].

c. Competitor's share of market and trend — This is derived data from (b) above.

d. Competitor's strengths and weaknesses — This represents a summary of key strong points and weak points for each competitor including [the company] as it participates in the market segment.

e. Competitor's strategies and priorities — This represents a summary of the strategies and priorities of each competitor including [the company].

f. *Competitor's current and future objectives* — This represents an identification of the objectives, both current and future, of the competitors and [the company] in relation to them.

g. *Competitor's cost and pricing factors* — i.e., in relation to [the company].

h. *Competitor's market, product and technology innovations and trends* — This represents an analysis of each competitor's market approach in relation to [the company] in the area of market, product, and technology innovations and trends.

i. *Competitor's current resources applied* — This represents a summary for each competitor including [the company] of the total resources applied (or relative resources in comparison to [the company]) in terms of manpower, facilities, IR and D, etc.

j. *Competitor's profits and trends* — This represents a comparison of [the company] to each of the competitors listed in (a) above.

k. *Competitors threat to [the company]* — This represents conclusions drawn from the data in (a) through (j) above relative to the threat that the competition poses to [the company].

l. *Key issues affecting success* — Based upon an analysis of (a) through (k) above, what key issues are identified that can cause a change in the [company] position relative to the competition?

"It is recognized that the information suggested in the above examples is difficult to obtain and the suggestion that it be analyzed and included in this section represents an ideal that may not be fully achievable. Nevertheless, the examples identify a listing of the key factors that have a bearing on the success of [the company] relative to the competition, and, where possible, information of this type should be sought out and uncovered for planning purposes. At the very least it should be indicated that we don't know when such is the case.

* * * *

"After the market and competitive analyses . . . are completed, the write-up should highlight the overall impact of the analysis relative to such factors as:

1. What is the general trend of the business area in terms of sales, competitiveness and position in the market?

2. What early signals can be noted in the analysis that suggest a change is taking place either in the market or competitive areas that will impact upon [the company] in either a positive or negative way? What seem to be the crucial alternatives for [the company]?

3. In the case of a new business analysis using this format, what signals are evident from the analysis that define a *particular* direction

(text continued on page 49)

Exhibit 15: Competitive Analysis Instructions — A Leisure Products Manufacturer

Competitive Analysis — Provide a concise description of any changes in the competitive situation since the last submission covering only major competitors (maximum top 3 to 4 factors). Important changes to be discussed would be a shift in market position, major strategy change, different product positioning or marketing emphasis. Succinctly update the key competition description in terms of overall and individual segment share or position; major strategies and marketing elements, such as pricing, product positioning, advertising and promotion (including advertising and promotion expenditures, where possible), distribution, consumer image, product and marketing strengths and weaknesses.

Highlight especially major factors that have helped or hindered [the company's] most recent performance and describe projected future competitive growth trends, market positions, major strategies, and expected areas of emphasis. For example:

- Competitor W, whose market share has been relatively constant for the past several years, has launched an aggressive advertising and promotion program to enhance its consumer franchise and sharply increase market share.

- Competitor X, who has been continuously losing share, has recently mounted an extensive campaign to turn the business around and regain its prior *dominant position* through the introduction of several new models, heavy advertising and promotion, and price cutting on selected existing models.

- Competitor Y has recently developed a revolutionary new patented electronic control safety device which severely threatens our position in this market segment.

- Competitor Z, who was a minor factor in the market last year, has bought company A, also a lesser competitor to [the company], and the combined resources of the new firm make it a major competitive force in a market previously dominated by [the company].

In projecting [the company] market share gains, it is especially important to focus on the competitor(s) from whom this share is to be gained. That's the purpose of Form 5148.

Market share data shall be shown on this form for [the company's] proprietary, private label (where appropriate), and major competition for the total market and for each major segment. Indicate the unit market share, actual or estimated, for the business unit and its three or four major competitors for the current and last year. Indicate the expected market shares during the plan period based upon [the company's] strategies of competition. Also indicate the sources and reliability of the market share data.

Suggested maximum length: 1-2 pages

Exhibit 15 (continued)

STRATEGIC PLAN
COMPETITION CHARACTERISTICS — MARKET SHARE

REPORTING COMPANY/DIVISION   GROUP/PROFIT CENTER   BUSINESS UNIT

| PRODUCT LINE | CURRENT YEAR ($ MIL.) | | % MARKET SHARE ON UNIT BASIS | | | | | | | | | | |
	TOTAL CORP. SALES	PRODUCT LINE SALES	YEAR −5 19___	YEAR −4 19___	YEAR −3 19___	YEAR −2 19___	YEAR −1 19___	CURR. YEAR 19___	BUDG. YEAR 19___	YEAR 2 19___	YEAR 3 19___	YEAR 4 19___	YEAR 5 19___
[The Company]	✕												
COMPETITION:													
			100%	100%	100%	100%	100%	100%	100%	100%	100%	100%	100%
SOURCES & RELIABILITY													

Form 5148 (Rev. 1/73)

Exhibit 16: External Analysis Form — A Container Company

STRATEGIC PLAN — 1975-1979

_____
(Division)

Key Competitors and Their Strategies

Competition	A	B	C	D
Name:				
Estimated sales volume and growth				
Product Line				
Customer Base				
Market size and growth				
Market share				
Technology				
Method chosen to compete				

Rank as most serious competition
  Now —
  1979 —				

Internal Evaluation —

What advantages do we have over
competitors?

What advantages does competition
have over us?

What can we do to counteract competitors strengths or to take
advantage of our strengths?

alternative among the several alternatives available?

4. What key and crucial elements of the information contained in the market and competitive analysis should be highlighted that will influence the judgments made in Section VII — Market Goals and Section VIII — Business Area Strategies?"

— An aerospace, electronics
and automative parts company
* * *

"1. *Markets*

a. The principal products and services being offered together with a breakdown of the principal customer markets in which they are sold.

b. The present and expected future rate of market growth.

c. Changes that are taking place in customer attitudes, needs and demands that might affect the product or service.

d. The price determination process in each market.

e. Expected trends in prices, margins, demand, supply.

f. Relative profitability of products offered.

"2. *Competition*

a. Principal competition in each product or service (both banks and non-banks).

b. Market share — past and expected future trend.

c. Competitors' strategies and their effect on us.

d. Trends in the competitive picture."

— A bank
* * *

Pinpointing the Key Considerations for Strategy Development

"Examination of a well-prepared fact base should immediately reveal a few key considerations — points of profit leverage changes in the marketplace, competitive strengths and weaknesses — that will provide management with a focus for strategy development. This section is not intended to be a laundry list of all factors affecting the business. If it were, it would merely repeat all the conclusions already stated in the fact base. The key is to select those critical factors that either point the way to improved profitability or that represent major constraints or threats to future growth and profits.

"The following checklist may be useful as a device for thinking about and then summarizing the major conclusions from the fact base that represent the key considerations for strategy development.

• Key profit leverage points, e.g., the more profitable products or segments of the business

• Market size and growth rates, e.g., emphasis on best opportunities

• Competitive environment, e.g., capacity utilization, pricing trends, number and size of competitors, or degree of integration

• Successful strategies of other competitors

• Trends in manufacturing technology, e.g., potential process breakthroughs, manufacturing techniques of major competitors

• Strengths and limitations of the division, e.g., marketing capability, R and D, product costs, raw material position, or management skills."

— A chemical company
* * *

"C. *Competitor Information*

A good appraisal, to provide a base for strategic and development planning, requires considerable information concerning competitive activity and strategy, including:

a) Determination as to whether competitors see the overall market segmented in the same way that you do, by analyzing the market segments and value packages of interest to each competitor;

b) The competitors' share of each market segment relative to yours;

c) Competitors' plans for new value packages, new markets, etc.;

d) Competitors' strengths, weaknesses, limitations, etc.;

Exhibit 17: External Analysis Form — A Diversified Industrial Products Company

MARKET/BUSINESS AUDIT

DATE _____

PRODUCT _____

DIVISION

1. Market Environment. _____

_____

2. Position in the Market: _____

_____

3. Marketing Considerations: _____

_____

4. Technical Considerations: _____

_____

5. Operational Considerations: _____

_____

6. Financial Considerations: _____

_____

e) Competitors' apparent strategy and reaction to competition.

Competitor information should be organized on a market segment basis, since competitors rarely compete equally across all market segments. Information can be obtained from many public sources, from common customers, and by the employment of consultants. The sources of information often are more available than expected but careful organization is required for its collection and analysis."

— An instrument and machinery manufacturer

* * *

"Inventory of Business Information

The inventory of business information is generally collected by a task force which draws on its experience, knowledge of the business, and calculated opinions about the business. They will generally interview other key people within the division and may go to external sources (e.g., marketing research consultants) to fill key information voids which are encountered.

The following pages include a model checklist which probes thoroughly the areas of markets, products, customer needs, competition, marketing capability and manufacturing.

An individual is assigned to prepare a consolidated statement summarizing all views and responses in a single set of answers. This consolidated statement is then submitted to each member of the task force to obtain confirmation or modification.

The task force and interviewing techniques exact a measure of involvement which will benefit the entire planning process. In many cases it will reveal weaknesses that have long been suspected but never isolated and clarified, potential strengths that have never been fully exploited, or opportunities that had not been previously identified.

The responses in the consolidated statement can be coded in terms of those which identify strengths, those which identify weaknesses, and those which indicate voids. In this manner it will serve as an outline for writing the analysis of current position.

Excerpts from Inventory of Business Information Checklist

Market Characteristics

The Customer
    Customer needs
    Customer profile

Product and Services
    Product definition
    Cost and pricing
    Service requirements
    Product plans

Competition

Marketing Capability
    Product management
    Market development
    Market intelligence
    Sales organization and coverage
    Marketing manpower and dealer development
    Advertising and sales promotion

Public relations
Division planning
Marketing management"
        — An industrial machinery company

Internal Analysis: Strengths and Weaknesses, Opportunities and Threats

The "inward look" at the business usually completes the overall appraisal needed for developing objectives and strategies. Guidance for evaluating strengths and weaknesses, opportunities and threats is not extensive in the planning documents studied, often consisting solely of definitions of the terms with some illustrative examples.

It would seem that this less numbers-oriented form of self-appraisal is more open to interpretation by the manager involved. Certainly the variety of explanations and instructions that mark previous portions of the situation analysis are not evident here. Yet there are some signposts along this path to provide guidance for the divisional planner or line executive.

For example, one planning manual offers "a helpful thought process" in identifying strengths and weaknesses: "Use acquisition analysis techniques," it suggests. "Imagine that you are buying the division as you have just described it. What are the unique resources of the organization that can be capitalized on to improve profitability and/or rate of growth? What are the cracks in the organization that hamper your ability to take advantage of opportunities or adequately meet competition? By 'standing back' and objectively viewing the present state of the division you will be able to isolate those factors which must be given consideration in future plans."

Another company's planning manual discusses the relationships between strengths and weaknesses, and opportunities and threats, more philosophically. It explains the relationships in the following manner.

"Strengths and weaknesses deal with the capabilities and/or capacity of the people, departmental functions, organizations, facilities, procedures, finances, etc. They may differ between segments of the business.

"The search for strengths and weaknesses tends to be an inward look, except that the standards of measurement should be related to the capabilities of competitors and the expectations of customers.

"Opportunities often result from a recognition of strengths. Weaknesses, on the other hand, should lead to the introduction of corrective development plans.

"Each strength or weakness is in a sense also an opportunity or threat if it is exploited by a division or a competitor. The distinction being emphasized, however, is that opportunities and threats represent advantageous or disadvantageous situations that could develop as a result of changes in strategy in competitor actions, or in the environment. The resulting list forms a checklist for the creation of strategies, and a checklist for the observance of changes which should trigger replanning or the initiation of contingency plans."

A food products manufacturer requires the following information to be included in the identification and evaluation of the business's capabilities and opportunities, explaining what is wanted as follows:

"1. Basic Capabilities — a listing of the skills, technologies, facilities, or other inherent abilities whether or not they are being used to their full potential (e.g., the unit or corporation may possess the ability to merchandise various food product lines even though it presently markets only one or two).

"2. List of Strengths — those products, services or activities that we currently make, provide or perform well — compared to our competition or our own standards (e.g., market share, management philosophy, etc.).

"3. List of Weaknesses — those products, services or activities that we currently make, provide or perform poorly — compared to our competition or our own standards. Weaknesses are *internal* and controllable (e.g., lack of

interfunctional communications, lack of sufficient information for decision making, etc.).

"4. List of Problems — a listing of current areas which are *external* and may or may not be partially controllable (e.g., raw material availability, FDA labeling regulations, etc.).

"5. List of Threats — a listing of potential *future* problems or weaknesses (e.g., legislative intervention, lack of new raw material sources, product recall, etc.).

"6. List of Opportunities — a listing of areas in which favorable sets of circumstances provide the potential for bettering the entity's position (e.g., diversification of product lines, development of productivity standards, cost reduction, etc.)."

The successful identification of opportunities, a bank's manual points out, is one of the most valuable attributes of good planning. It further explains that the successful elimination of problems should be considered an opportunity, if "you share these problems with competitors and they are unable to solve these same problems."

A number of companies simply define the concepts involved in this self-analysis, although some go on to furnish illustrative examples. Some of these definitions and examples are given below.

"Strengths are advantages, uniquenesses and exclusives. Weaknesses are encumbrances and vulnerabilities.

"Opportunities and needs are ways of capitalizing on strengths or converting weaknesses into strengths."

            — An industrial machinery company

*   *   *

"An opportunity is typically a broad-based chance to fulfill an unmet need. This need can be the result of a new development or simply a modification of existing demand.

"Examples might be:

"Per-capita meat consumption, both foreign and domestic, will continue to rise in excess of population growth.

SWOPT Items

The purpose of this subsection is to uncover and evaluate additional conditions and situations which were not discussed in the previous plan sections and which must be taken into account when developing goals and strategies. Examples might be: restrictions imposed by the current financial position; personnel capabilities, weaknesses or expected departures; opportunities opened by new or improved resources, an unusually favorable reputation or close relationship with customers or consumers, etc.

The following list of definitions is provided to show the derivation of "SWOPT."

. STRENGTHS: Things we are good at and should make the most of.

. WEAKNESSES: Things we do poorly and should correct or avoid. The *internal* things that keep us from reaching our goals.

. OPPORTUNITIES: Things we could or should be doing, but are not. Includes possible solutions to our important problems.

. PROBLEMS: External things that keep us from reaching our goals. Obstacles we must overcome.

. THREATS: Those things that might happen if preventative measures are not taken.

Another reason for including the above definitions is to stimulate thinking. Often one considers a planning situation only in terms of "problems" or only in terms of internal "strengths and weaknesses." But a problem, looked at from other viewpoints, might be an opportunity, or an internal weakness.

Although the thinking process involved may look at the same situation from different viewpoints, the written results should not be repetitious. Items adequately covered in earlier sections of the "Current Situation and Outlook" should not be repeated. Usually no item should be discussed under more than one SWOPT category. Find the most accurate or suitable viewpoint and discuss the subject once.

Much more detail may be developed in the SWOPT process than should be included in the written plan. Do not list the obvious items. Identify those with the most profit potential or leverage and concentrate on these. Include only those items which help explain strategic and tactical decisions. The statements should be terse and brief. They should identify the major, fundamental factors but not all of their symptoms and previous causes.

Discussion of SWOPT items, without the investigation and development of "hard facts" for the other sections of the Current Situation and Outlook, may seem to be an "easy way out." But it will usually result in a shallow analysis that "fails to get at the heart of the problems."

— A tire and rubber producer

"Our product-tolerance measurement system conforms to the FDA requirement and thus offers potential marketability to our less sophisticated competitors.

"The opening of Chinese trade offers a potentially significant market for our low cost-high margin protein substitutes.

"A threat is any factor (or combination of several factors) which has the potential of destroying your existing competitive position.

Consequently, it forces you to take remedial action for self-preservation.

"Examples of threats are:

"The unforeseen entry into commodity-feed processing of Competitor X and the potential price erosion therein.

"New technology requiring a large capital commitment has been already initiated by Competitors X and Y.

"Our primary raw material sources are concentrated in the Midwest and therefore are subject to similar production and harvest problems."

— A diversified company

Exhibits 18-22 are forms used by companies to explore these elements of internal appraisal. As noted, specific businesses or industries may direct attention to special concerns that are significant to the success of their various enterprises. Thus the performance appraisal a bank asks for in its internal analysis requirements includes not only an´ appraisal of the division's staff, but that of related activities within the bank which extend or constrain that planning unit's activities. "Those variables which have or might have a significant impact on unit performance should be evaluated," it advises.

Some "issues-oriented" companies seek to identify in their internal appraisals strategic issues relevant to the fulfillment of the business mission. One company explains that these issues can be classified this way.

"1. A significant *existing satisfactory situation* that needs protecting or developing.

"2. A serious *existing fault* that must be corrected.

"3. A major *future opportunity* that can be profitably exploited.

"4. A dire *future threat* that must be avoided or ameliorated."

(text continued on page 57)

Exhibit 18: Internal Analysis Form, with Illustrations — A Recreational Products Company

STRATEGIC PLAN 1975–1979
Business Unit A

SITUATION ANALYSIS

Date: June, 1974

	OPPORTUNITIES	**PROBLEMS**
RAPIDLY GROWING DIVISION	GREATER PROFIT AND REVENUE OPPORTUNITIES.	LARGE WORKING CAPITAL REQUIREMENTS. HARD PRESSED TO KEEP PLANT CAPACITY EXPANSION PROGRAMS UP WITH SALES. DEALER AND DISTRIBUTOR GROWTH HAMPERED BY THEIR WORKING CAPITAL LIMITATIONS.
DIVISION RANKS 3RD IN SIZE IN INDUSTRY	CAN BETTER ATTRACT NEW AND LARGER SHARE OF BUSINESS FROM MAJOR NATIONAL ACCOUNTS. MANUFACTURING AND ENGINEERING STRENGTHS AND EFFICIENCES BRING PRODUCTS TO MARKET COMPETITIVELY PRICED.	ACQUISITION CANDIDATES HARD TO QUALIFY DUE TO DIVISION'S DOMINANT MARKET POSITION. PRESENT PLANTS AT MAXIMUM CAPACITY.

Exhibit 19: Internal Analysis Form — A Container Manufacturer

STRATEGIC PLAN — 1975-1979

_____

(Division)

Major Opportunities and Threats

Major Threat	Possible effect threat could have upon operating conditions or profitability.
Major Opportunities	Possible direction that could be pursued to take advantage of opportunity.

STRATEGIC PLAN — 1975-1979

_____

(Division)

Major Strengths and Weaknesses
(as related to the external environment
and the strategic charter)

Major Strengths	Strategies and action plans which will capitalize on or take advantage of such strengths.
Major Weaknesses	Strategies and action plans which will improve weaknesses or compensate risks or problems involved with weaknesses.

Exhibit 20: Internal Analysis Form — A Paperboard Manufacturer

1975-1980 PLAN

IMPACT OF KEY OPPORTUNITIES OR RISKS

Description	Probability of occurrence	Most likely impact			Comments
		Revenues	Profit before tax	Capital employed	

Exhibit 21: Internal Analysis Form — A Food Processing Company

STRENGTHS AND WEAKNESSES:

	STRENGTHS			WEAKNESSES
Function or Skill	Unique (1)	Among the Best (2)	Above Average (3)	Average/Below (4)
R and D				
Supply				
Processing				
Physical distribution				
Marketing				
Consumer franchise				
Sales				
Trade relations				
Managerial				
Financial				
Land availability				
Other				

Product-Line Analysis

To complete the analysis, many planning guides call for an appraisal of the company's individual products or product lines. A thorough breakdown of the unit's product lines may be a regular item in the appraisal portion of the divisional plan, or sometimes the focus of a particular planning cycle.

A first step in strategic planning, according to one manufacturer's manual, is "the identification of the distinguishable product lines that make up the business of the operating unit. An in-depth analysis of the total future operating environment for each product line is then required before developing a strategic plan."

A diversified company wants to know the degree of product leadership for each of its units' major products, and in what respects (quality, performance, packaging, brand image, price, value, etc.) each is superior, equal or inferior to competition. In addition, its instructions state:

"Indicate for each major product its degree of maturity. Most products go through a typical life cycle which begins with slow growth during the introductory period, followed by rapid sales growth, then slower growth, maturity and eventual decline. If a product is considered mature or declining, discuss the steps being taken to improve or replace the product."

Among the data (historical and forecast) required for each product line by an electronic components company are separate schedules for each of the following:

Market size and growth rate
Markets by major competitors (estimated current revenues)
Product-line revenues and growth rate
Product-line revenues – graphs
Product-line revenue share and market share
Gross margin by product line
Income and ROS by product line

Average net assets and ROI by product line
Units and prices.

Some other approaches to this type of information are shown in Exhibits 23-25.

Evaluation of Previous Plan

The epilogue to the divisional self-appraisal – but not a fixed requirement for all plans – is the analysis or evaluation of previous plans. Since most financial formats call for the figures of previous years, simple comparisons are easily made (see Exhibits 26 and 27). Some plans, however, propose in addition a more qualitative review of former estimates against present realities.

A guide for a staff corporate unit's plan, for example, reads as follows:

"Review of Performance and Plan Changes

"The purpose of this section is two-fold: to point out (1) any differences between actual performance and planned performance for the current year; and (2) any changes that have been made in future plans or programs since the last formal plan revision.

"Variances or changes to both quantitative and nonquantitative objectives, goals, strategies and programs should be considered and shown in this section with particular emphasis on the latter.

"Quantitative changes generally will be related to the department's performance against numerically measurable goals, e.g., personnel goals, budget goals, etc.

"Nonquantitative changes and variances generally will be related to significant changes in the department's overall major objectives, strategies and environmental forecasts. Changes in the initiation or completion dates of projects should also be pointed out and explained, as should the changes in the scope or nature of the projects.

"The reviews of performance and plan changes that are included in each department plan should cover the entire period since the

(text continued on page 65)

Exhibit 22: Internal Analysis Form, with Illustrations — A Food Processor

POSITION/POTENTIAL GRAPH

PROFIT CENTER : _____

SUBSTANTIAL GROWTH
AND PROFIT
OPPORTUNITIES

STRONG	PRODUCT/CONCEPT A PRODUCT/CONCEPT E		PRODUCT/CONCEPT F	MODERATE GROWTH AND PROFIT OPPOR-TUNITIES
[Company] MODERATE POTENTIAL	PRODUCT/CONCEPT C	PRODUCT/CONCEPT B		
WEAK			PRODUCT/CONCEPT D	LIMITED GROWTH AND PROFIT OPPOR-TUNITIES

SUBSTANTIAL   MODERATE   LOW

INDUSTRY ATTRACTIVENESS

Exhibit 22 (continued)

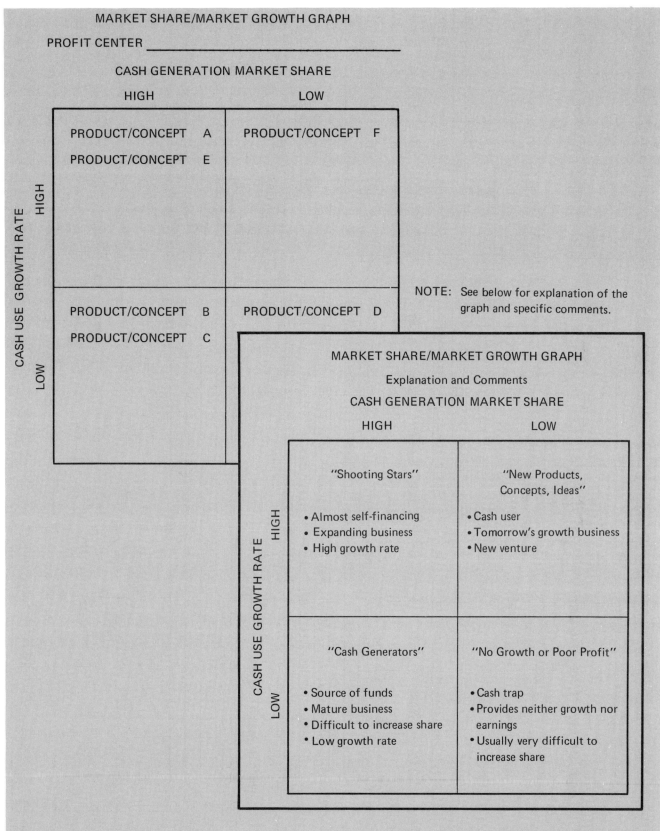

MARKET SHARE/MARKET GROWTH GRAPH

PROFIT CENTER _____

CASH GENERATION MARKET SHARE

	HIGH	LOW
HIGH	PRODUCT/CONCEPT A PRODUCT/CONCEPT E	PRODUCT/CONCEPT F
LOW	PRODUCT/CONCEPT B PRODUCT/CONCEPT C	PRODUCT/CONCEPT D

CASH USE GROWTH RATE

NOTE: See below for explanation of the graph and specific comments.

MARKET SHARE/MARKET GROWTH GRAPH

Explanation and Comments

CASH GENERATION MARKET SHARE

	HIGH	LOW
HIGH	"Shooting Stars" • Almost self-financing • Expanding business • High growth rate	"New Products, Concepts, Ideas" • Cash user • Tomorrow's growth business • New venture
LOW	"Cash Generators" • Source of funds • Mature business • Difficult to increase share • Low growth rate	"No Growth or Poor Profit" • Cash trap • Provides neither growth nor earnings • Usually very difficult to increase share

CASH USE GROWTH RATE

Exhibit 23: Product-Line Forecast, with Illustrations — A Capital Goods, Automotive and Consumer Products Company

1979 – PRODUCT-LINE FORECAST

Forecast Data in Thousands of Constant 1974 U.S. Dollars
(Local Currency)

[Name]
Division, Plant or Subsidiary

[Name]
Product Line

165
Number

	1973		1974		Target Years 1977		1979	
Breakdown of Sales and Profit*	Sales	Profit	Sales	Profit	Sales	Profit	Sales	Profit
Present product line	$ 2500	$ 500	$ 2700	$ 540	$ 2700	$ 540	$ 2700	$ 540
External factors affecting present product line								
Market for [product line] will grow at 3.0% per year in units or constant dollars.								
Imports of lower cost [product line] from Japan will increase competition and reduce [the company] market share.					$ 200	$ 40	$ 380	$ 76
OSHA will probably require safety devices on [product line] — in anticipation customers					(150)	(30)	(320)	(64)
will buy from competition since [the company] doesn't have such a device.					(95)	(19)	(200)	(40)
Metric designs of competition are compatible with both U.S. and European requirements.					(50)	(10)	(106)	(21)
External Factor Subtotal					$ (95)	$ (19)	$ (246)	$ (49)
Results of Action Programs								
Corporate Pul-Lift Programs					$ 388	$ 78	$ 876	$ 175
Improve hoist distribution system					57	11	120	24
Action Program Subtotal					$ 445	$ 89	$ 996	$ 199
Product-Line History and Objective	$ 2500	$ 500	$ 2700	$ 540	$ 3050	$ 610	$ 3450	$ 690
Standard Profit		34%		35%		33%		34%
*Line 62 Profit		20%		20%		20%		20%
Market Share	20%		20%		21%		22%	

Exhibit 24: Product-Line Analysis Form — A Manufacturer of Industrial Products

Product-Line or Business-Unit Fact Sheet

	1972	1973	1974	1975	1976
1. Size of market					
2. Percent growth rate-past					
3. Percent growth rate-future					
4. Your sales volume					
5. Percent growth rate-past					
6. Percent growth rate-future					
7. Your share of market					
8. Your largest competitors' share					
9. Return on sales					
10. Return on assets					
11. Assets employed					
12. "Strategic expense" dollars					
13. Capital expenditures					
14. Sales per employee					
15. Assets per employee					
16. Inventory turnover					
17. Receivable DSO					
18. Fixed asset turnover					
19. Total asset turnover					

Where facts are not available use your best estimate. If it is not possible to estimate, indicate n.a. (not available). Where asset breakdown by product line is not feasible, make reasonable estimates or allocations.

Exhibit 25: Product-Line Analysis Form — A Diversified Industrial Products Company

MARKET/BUSINESS AUDIT
PRODUCT PERFORMANCE

DATE _____
DIVISION _____

PRODUCT IDENTIFICATION Name and SIC Number (List by Priority)	FISCAL YEAR	PRODUCT MATURITY				MARKET			BUSINESS					PERFORMANCE MEASURES			
		START-UP	GROWTH	MATURE	DECLINE	Market Size ($000)	Annual Market Growth (%)	Product Sales Volume ($000)	Assets Employed ($000)	Current Assets Employed ($000)	Earnings Before Tax ($000)	Cash Returned ($000)	Return on Sales (%)	Asset Turn-over	Return on Assets (%)	Cash Return on Assets (%)
DIVISION TOTAL	73															
	74															
	75															
	76															
	77															
	78															
Product No. 1	73															
	74															
	75															
	76															
	77															
	78															
Product No. 2	73															
	74															
	75															
	76															
	77															
	78															
Product No. 3	73															
	74															
	75															
	76															
	77															
	78															
Product No. 4	73															
	74															
	75															
	76															

Exhibit 26: Form for Evaluation of Previous Plan — A Tire Manufacturer

COMPARISON OF PREVIOUS YEAR'S ACTUAL PERFORMANCE WITH THE LAST TWO YEARS' PLANS AND COMPARISON OF CURRENT PLAN WITH THE PREVIOUS YEAR'S PLAN — 1974 PLAN

	1973 Est.	'72 Plan For '73	Actual Percent '72 Plan	'73 Plan For '73	Actual Percent '73 Plan	'73 Plan For '74	'74 Plan For '74	Percent Change 1974 to 1973
			1973				1974	
NET SALES								
NET TRADE SALES								
COST OF SALES								
SELLING AND GENERAL ADMINISTRATION								
OPERATING INCOME								
PRETAX INCOME								
CAPITAL EXPENDITURES								
NET CAPITAL EMPLOYED								
ENROLLMENT								
RATIOS: Operating Income/Sales								
Pretax Income/Sales								
Operating Income/Net Capital								
Pretax Income/Net Capital								
Net Sales/Employee								

Exhibit 27: Form for Evaluation of Previous Plan — An Industrial Machinery Company

REVIEW OF PRIOR PLANS

_____ Division

A.   PLANNED RESULTS ($ Millions)

	1976				1978		
	74-78 LRBP	75-79 LRBP	76-80 LRBP		74-78 LRBP	75-79 LRBP	76-80 LRBP
Sales							
Net Income							
ROCE							

B.   MILESTONE GOALS FROM 1975-1979 LRBP

1.

2.

3.

4.

(etc.)

Changes to long-range business plans are a significant indicator of change in the division's internal and external operating environment. Compare planned results from the 1974-1978 LRBP with the 1975-1979 LRBP and with planned results from the 1976-1980 LRBP for the years 1976 and 1978 in terms of sales (billings), net income (after tax), and ROCE.

Goals are specific statements of results to be achieved, and the timing of their achievement. They may be of the statistical or milestone type. Under B. MILESTONE GOALS FROM 1975-1979 LRBP duplicate the listing of milestone goals from your 1975-1979 LRBP. At the end of each milestone goal add one of the following key words (in capital letters) to describe the current status of each 1975-1979 LRBP milestone goal.

ACHIEVED: goal has been reached.

DELETED: goal is no longer appropriate.

ACTIVE: goal, as stated, remains appropriate but has not been achieved.

CHANGED: goal has been restated either in terms of results to be achieved or timing of achievement.

last written department plan was formally approved and issued. Normally, this should be an annual review made in the fourth quarter of the year. A midyear review also is suggested to track progress toward plan goals."

A broader view on the evaluation of previous strategies is taken in another planning guide: "It is rare that a business requires a completely new strategic direction. A valuable input to the process is the analysis of the results of previous strategies. A determination should be made as to whether previous strategies have been improving the competitive posture and whether they are valid for the new environmental, market and competitive situations."

Managers of an industrial products firm are directed to evaluate the impact of subsequent events on previous strategies. They are also asked to indicate what changes they are proposing in the strategy they are currently submitting to reflect the changes that have taken place in the business environment.

Objectives, Goals

The voluminous data accumulated in the previous portions of the planning exercise are the background from which the objectives and goals emerge. Objectives and goals, in turn, are the forerunners of the strategy section of the plan — the means of accomplishment.

Any discussion of objectives and goals, however, must confront the semantics problem that afflicts this part of the planning process. Many companies attempt to clarify or separate the two concepts in their planning instructions, giving rise to a plethora of definitions (see box on page 67). The explanatory comments in several guides suggest differences in the basic nature of these concepts.

Considered in the classic definition of being conceptual and long-term in nature, objectives are generally understood to be "declarations of purpose" that express management's fundamental intentions toward pursuing and accomplishing its mission. They do not necessarily change from plan to plan unless there are basic changes in the business or in its environment.

Goals are defined as the statements of specifics to buttress the objectives. They are usually quantified — setting targets, dates, milestones. They are, as one document describes them, "finite and measureable." Very often goals are identified with the individual who will be responsible for achieving them.

These concepts are presented in the planning manual of a paper company in this manner:

" 'Objectives' and 'goals' lie on a continuum of intended results. Objectives are at the broad and long-range end, while goals are at the specific and short-term end. The words 'objectives' and 'goals' are chosen simply to indicate the relative end of the continuum on which the intended result lies."

Lacking a single accepted definition of each of these terms, many companies use the two terms interchangeably, or use one or the other exclusively. (Some firms also refer to "targets.") Since one company's objective may be another company's goal, the discussion which follows treats the two together.

The principal objectives or goals to be specified in the divisional plans are financial and marketing targets. Other areas of business activity are also specified in some plans.

In the financial area, the following goals are most often called for:

Net Sales
Return on investment
Net income (sometimes also as percent of net sales)
Gross profit (sometimes also as percent of net sales)
Net profit
Return on assets and sales
Cumulative and/or cash flow
Total capital expenditures
Operating investment
Earnings growth

Marketing goals are usually stated in terms of market share, industry ranking, penetration of new markets, introduction of new products (and phasing out of old ones), sales volume.

Other objectives or goals suggested for divisional plans, depending on the company or industry, are: cost reduction, product improvement, safety measures, facility and manpower changes, and research and development.

One of the surprises many planning directors and top executives find in the first go-around of a new planning process is the number of objectives that divisions can turn in. Quite a number of companies have, therefore, placed constraints on the *number* of objectives which may be submitted, and the number of pages discussing them.

Characteristics, Criteria

Perhaps the criterion found most frequently among the documents describing objectives or goals is *measurability*. This appears to be the characteristic desired to head off fantasies and nail down realities. Numbers, rates, ratios, percentages — all are demanded as measures of divisional goals.

The next most-wanted attribute is *achievability*. Hard realism must now take over: "No motherhood statements," cautions one firm. The setting of too-modest objectives or goals is also deemed undesirable.

Other desired characteristics of objectives or goals are specific timetables with dates and milestones. Many goals instructions also ask for the assignment of responsibility at this stage.

The following desired characteristics are spelled out in one manual:

"1. The overall objective should be of a long-term nature, two or more fiscal years. The objective should extend out far enough that it can be expressed in terms of a meaningful business result. For example, a new product development should extend out to the point of a meaningful sales level, not just to the point of introduction to the market. The latter is a subobjective or milestone.

"2. The objective should have high priority and a bearing on the future of the division. The impact of success or failure should be consequential.

"3. As a result of the above characteristics, each objective will normally stay on the selected list until its full completion. It is recognized that changes in the measure of completion and in milestones will occur as the program progresses.

"4. Revenue, orders, market share, production rate, or an efficiency measure such as productivity or scrap rate, are typical measures of completion. Some, such as customer

Exhibit 28: Examples of Objectives — A Division of an Agricultural Equipment Company

---

Air Pollution Control Division

*IMAGE: Become a recognized leader in the development and application of air pollution control equipment in the U.S. marketplace.

*INDUSTRY POSITION: Obtain 30 percent of the served market for air pollution control equipment in the U.S. marketplace.

*VERTICAL INTEGRATION: Increase percentage of value added/cost of sales to 60 percent.

*ROI: Achieve an ROI for the division of 20 percent.

*INTERNATIONAL SALES: Achieve 20 percent of annual sales volume from international markets.

How Companies Define <u>Objectives</u> and <u>Goals</u>

Many of the manuals in this study expend a good deal of effort in an attempt to clarify the meanings of *objectives* and *goals* as used in the company's planning process. It remains, however, a rather elusive ideal, as shown in one manual's explanation of its definition of *goal*:

"The previous edition [of this manual] made a distinction between *objective* and *goal* which has been abandoned because of the resulting confusion."

The following definitions are taken from planning documents submitted for this report.

"*Objectives*. The broad, continuing business aims or purposes which guide the management of the business and which are generally expected to pertain over a period of years.

"*Goals*. The major, specific milestones or end results to be accomplished which will achieve or be a step toward achievement of an objective. Goals should be time oriented, measurable and challenging."

*   *   *

"An objective is defined as 'a temporary hypothesis regarding a very desirable future result that cannot be predicted with accuracy, which can be achieved through your efforts.' . . . Objectives and goals are synonymous."

*   *   *

"*Objective*. Brief statement of qualitative results or achievements that are desired.

"*Goals*. Very specific, quantifiable targets which are derived from objectives. These should contain specific percentage figures, ratios, dollar amounts, and/or dates."

*   *   *

"The *goal* is a statement of what business we are in. Firms make profits doing something — the something is the business definition or goal. Some prefer to define goals as the mission.

"*Objectives* are the measuring devices used along the way, including ROI, share of market, absolute sales, or profit as a percentage of sales. Some objectives are nonfinancial, such as employee opportunities and community and social responsibility."

*   *   *

"*Objectives*. . . . Objectives represent declara-

tions of purpose and, as such, define the desired end result of future activities. Objectives should be of a continuing nature and establish the broad framework within which the division or subsidiary intends to achieve its mission.

"*Goals*. . . . The divisonal or subsidiary goals should represent quantitative targets designed to achieve their objectives and should be accompanied by specific target dates."

*   *   *

"*Objectives and Goals*. A statement of very long-term (10-year) company objectives and inter-mediate-range (one- to five-year) goals setting forth specific, realizable targets. Objectives should delineate in broad terms both the *direction* and *rate* of future growth. Specific goals within this framework may deal with such factors as size, sales or profit growth, functions you perform (or customer needs you fulfill), product line, customer or supplier dependency, market position, new product development, and other critical aspects of your business."

*   *   *

"Objectives are broad, enduring statements of purpose which impel a business to make the best use of its resources, capabilities and opportunities.

"Goals are specific statements of results to be achieved, and the timing of their achievement."

*   *   *

"*Objectives*. Each objective statement should identify what shall be measured (the result), the yardstick (measurement or indicator), the target (value and timetable), and who is responsible for its accomplishment. In general, objectives should identify longer-term targets — beyond the horizon of the planning year — as it is to be expected that (1) basic objectives at the division or affiliate level generally remain valid from one year to the next, and (2) short-term (one-year) plans generally require the focus of longer-term purpose.

"*Goals*. Goals will be identified for each objective. The goal, as we use the term, identifies the short-term (next year's) target for each objective."

*   *   *

"Objectives are the quantitative targets of the business — primarily earnings and their relation-ship to investment — sales and sales mix."

acceptance, may be more qualitative, but the emphasis should be to find a measurable quantity.

"5. Over the full life span of an objective, the division's key management resources spanning the total top organization structure are likely to be involved.

"6. Each overall objective will have a number of subobjectives or milestones which are due for completion within the fiscal year and, through the medium of the quarterly review, will give advance warning of difficulty in completion of the fiscal year program."

A life insurance company issues this check list for objectives and goals:

"1. Results Objectives and Goals

a. Do they tie in with the major measures of performance of the division and, when achieved, contribute to fulfilling the company's basic mission?

b. Have they been put in perspective by comparing them to the past performance in that area?

c. Are they sufficiently specific and quantitatively expressed so that accomplishments can be measured against objectives with such accuracy that no difference of opinion will arise between the division head and his department head over whether or not the objectives have actually been achieved?

d. Are they ambitious enough?

e. Are they attainable?

f. Do they generate improvements in performance?

"2. Means Objectives and Goals

a. Do they spell out the key activities that need to be performed in order to achieve each results objective?

b. Do they set specific and quantitative targets for each key activity?

c. Do they undertake the main activities in the correct order of priority?

d. Do they describe all key changes in sufficient detail as a first step towards controlling the process of implementing the major improvements?"

Top-Down Divisional Objectives

Most corporate objectives issued in the planning process (see page 22) are broad enough for the divisions to formulate their own objectives and goals within the corporate framework. A food processor explains the rationale of this process:

"Top management should provide preliminary or tentative organization objectives as guidelines within which divisional, functional and program objectives can be developed. As a matter of fact, it is really impossible to establish good objectives at subordinate levels unless and until objectives have been clarified at higher levels becuase an objective is not valid unless it supports the objectives of the next echelon."

Some companies, however, interpret the setting of division objectives as a function of the higher corporate level. Accordingly, division objectives are handed down by corporate headquarters; the division's role is to furnish goals and strategies and programs toward their accomplishment (see Exhibit 29). The division is thus relieved of this part of the planning process, but usually has some recourse against having to accept the issued objectives.

A leisure products manufacturer, for example, has a procedure whereby the division may state its reasons for nonconcurrence with the objectives and guidelines laid down by the executive office. The procedure also provides for the business unit's analysis of how it will meet these objectives, or how it will modify them based on the opportunities or challenges the unit sees in the marketplace.

The juggling of objectives between organizational levels can disturb the planning system if sequences and priorities are not spelled out. Conflicts, if any occur, are usually resolved at corporate reviews.

Setting Goals

Not many companies in this study issue explicit directions for the unit to follow in establishing its goals. Numerical goals are arrived at, to a large extent, through study of the data

Exhibit 29: Objectives, Goals Form — A Diversified Industrial Products Company

	1st Year's Goal	3rd Year's Goal	Priority
DIVISIONAL GOALS			
OBJECTIVE 1			
a. Management development	— — — —	— — — —	
b. Quality and effectiveness of management	— — — —	— — — —	
OBJECTIVE 2			
a. Sales volume			
b. Market share			
c. New product development			
d. New market development			
OBJECTIVE 3			
a. Identify high-growth market for potential acquisition			
OBJECTIVE 4			
a. Return on sales			
b. Return on assets			
c. Cash return on assets			
d. Maintain strict financial controls	— — — —	— — — —	
OBJECTIVE 5			
a. Recognize changing economic conditions and redeploy affected assets	— — — —	— — — —	
OBJECTIVE 6			
a. Sales per employee			
b. Sales per dollar of asset employed			

Exhibit 30: Objectives, Goals Instructions — A Mutual Life Insurance Company

Statements of objectives and their corresponding goals are best formulated by starting the statement with an action verb, followed by a noun, followed by a concrete measure.

Examples:

OBJECTIVES		GOALS
A. Do something	by	when
B. Lower something	to	x%
C. Keep unit cost	at	x amount
D. Do something	to obtain	$ savings
E. Continue trend in x	in order to have	y go down z%

The importance of having objectives with specifically identifiable and corresponding goals is apparent when measuring and reporting progress. For a manager to judge or be judged on his department's accomplishments, he himself must know with certainty whether an objective and its goals have been achieved.

---

prepared in the situation analysis. A tire manufacturer suggests a procedure for its divisions to derive future sales and profits numbers for each existing product line:

"1. First look at the anticipated industry growth associated with each product. . . .

"2. The next step would logically be to determine what share of market your division can set as the objective based upon all of the information previously assembled in [historical sales and profits section]. . . .

"3. You should next evaluate the reasonableness of the industry forecast and/or your volume product sales objectives by considering some of the appropriate social and political factors mentioned in [historical sales and profits section], and the plans of the [company] research groups contained in the [company's technological forecast publication].

"4. The fourth step should be to convert the volume estimates for each product into dollar sales by calculating the historical [data] and then projecting average dollar sales per unit

(pound) to arrive at total dollar sales. (This may not be necessary if dollar sales were derived directly.)

"5. Finally, you should determine total gross profit based upon an estimate of gross profit as a percent to sales."

Whereas financial and market objectives and goals are most prevalent for divisions, they are difficult to establish for corporate staff units. Sometimes only expected spending levels are sought for these cost centers, but many companies issue specific guides for these units or else ask for more qualitative objectives. Goals should "reflect responsibilities to the corporation," a glass producer's manual states, and asks staff units to think in terms of how they may better serve other divisions. A bank suggests that the personnel department, for example, might set goals on turnover rates or unfilled requisitions.

Some of the problems involved in setting goals in corporate staff units of a corporation are discussed by a rubber products firm.

"The areas in which goals should be established for a support department are much more difficult to determine than the goal areas of a profit center. This is because the accounting system of a profit center already defines, measures and reports actual results in important profit center areas such as sales, income and return on investment. In a support department all that is usually measured by the accounting or data processing systems are the expenses, which are not a measure of the desired ends or results. Goals for output and effectiveness are left to each department to define and measure for itself. Nevertheless, goals and goal measuring techniques should be established, wherever possible, for all of the most important key success factors. . . . More specifically, measures of the productivity or effectiveness of the support division must be defined. Then the past and current levels of these goals must be obtained so that realistic levels of the planned goals for future periods can be specified. These planned levels should be based on (1) the strategies, policies, projects and time schedules selected; (2) the resources available; (3) the specified assumptions about the future conditions and environment; and (4) the assumption that the plan implementation will be effectively and efficiently managed. . . .

"The 'desired' (or reaching) goal level must be based on what is needed to meet the overall corporate objectives and what is believed possible if new approaches, strategies and techniques are developed. This belief must be founded in judgment, optimism and a knowledge of what the best of other companies have been able to do under similar circumstances."

Closing the Gap

Planned or forecast goal levels do not always meet the desired objectives of the corporation, thereby creating what has been termed the "planning gap." Obviously, closing the gap becomes a major preoccupation in formulating the strategic section of the long-range plan.

Choices and decisions have to be made at this point on how to deal with the discrepancy: Can the gap best be closed by internal programs or by external growth? What is the probability of accomplishing the results needed? Should the goal be changed? "The degree to which the planning gap is closed from year to year provides a measure of the planning effectiveness of the department," states one of the study manuals.

Another company advises its divisions first to improve sales and profits "by fully utilizing current resources and by overcoming current limitations instead of seeking new opportunities at the beginning of the planning cycle." Then, if a gap exists between goals for the future and expected results from existing operations, "close the gap from new product or market development or through acquisitions and mergers. The benefit of this approach," it goes on, "is that profits may be increased by giving the proper attention to existing activities in your long-range plans, instead of spending an undue amount of effort on more exciting, but more risky, new activities."

The objectives and goals section of the division plan cannot be fully concluded until the means for closing the gap have been developed.

Strategies

The sequence of developing a long-range plan, starting with the fact base of the situation analysis, goes on to the value judgments necessary to set goals and objectives, and culminates in the challenge of developing and implementing strategies — the heart of the process. This is "how we are going to get there."

Planning manuals and other corporate guides often expend much effort in explaining both the hard realism and imaginative creativity needed for developing strategies. Balancing the two approaches is a delicate maneuver. One planning handbook declares: "Successful formulation and execution of a strategy ordinarily requires rigor, experimentation, questioning of old methods, exploring unfamiliar environments, facing up to strengths, weaknesses, opportunities and threats, forcing change, and acceptance of uncertainties."

Developing strategies is widely agreed to be

difficult, and some of the corporate guide documents attempt to help their planners through this process. Several of the more educationally oriented manuals, in fact, contain extensive expositions of strategy. Many more, however, focus instead on the documented format they require for the action programs and projects. The latter, of course, are more easily explained and formalized.

The rather broad descriptions of strategy discussed in the planning guides suggest several procedures for managers to consider. They are advised, for example, to maximize the strengths and minimize the weaknesses of the division; and to take advantage of the opportunities afforded by the competition's strengths and weaknesses. One guide suggests that the key factors for success in the division be analyzed as a prelude to strategy formulation.

Another useful method proposed is to identify key issues stemming from the planning effort already completed. An analysis of the competition's strategy, for instance, is often a determinant of the divisional strategy selected.

A general approach to strategy development is suggested by a paper company:

"1. Create several alternative courses of action (strategies) to achieve the objective.

"2. For each alternative strategy identify the future decision points and the choices available at each decision point, the uncertain events and their possible outcomes, the resource requirements, and the potential payoffs. In addition, those problems of each strategy that require further investigation should be identified.

"3. Evaluate each alternative strategy on the basis of its expected outcome. Select the 'best' alternative and state it clearly and completely.

"4. Evaluate the selected strategy and the original objectives in greater detail for overall acceptability with regard to risks and the availability of satisfactory contingency plans. If the result is unacceptable, the original objectives should be revised, or additional strategies should be formulated and evaluated.

"5. Develop the selected strategy to the level of detail required for the initiation of efficient, effective and timely implementation (i.e., develop goals, tactics, schedules, etc.), and identify the most critical actions and events. The development and evaluation of this detail may result in adjustments to the basic strategy, and perhaps even to the objectives."

Other considerations mentioned in the guides for developing strategies comment on the need for consistency. Primarily, the strategies must be consistent with corporate mission and objectives. They should also present no conflict internally in the organization, and externally should be in tune with the changing environment.

Documenting Strategies

Strategies implement objectives, as action programs implement strategies. Not all companies make sharp delineations among these three concepts. Indeed, they are so closely interrelated that difficulties arise in getting division managers to interpret each properly. Thus one food company advises its managers:

"In the past, some strategic plans have lacked substance and credibility. Strategies are the heart of the plans and we would like them to be more fully documented than in the past. . . .

"By way of example, we would not consider it a strategy if the product manager for widgits tells us that his plan is 'to launch a major consumer marketing program to expand market share in widgits.' This is an objective rather than a strategy. A real strategy should explain what kind of marketing leverage will be used and what kind of positioning against customers and competitors will be made. It should also indicate such things as where the widgit will be produced and whether increased plant capacity is required, when the program will be launched, what support services will be required, who will be responsible for executing the various steps of the plan, and so on. If some of these variables are not presently known, the timetable for developing the answers should be set out."

Exhibit 31: Strategy Summary Form — A Bank

STRATEGY SUMMARY

1.   ACTION STRATEGY — What is it?

2.   RELATED LONG-RUN OBJECTIVE — Why is this strategy being proposed, and how will it help reach an objective?

3.   STATE OF DEVELOPMENT — Is it an existing, improved, or new strategy?

4.   CRITERIA FOR STRATEGY SELECTION — Was this strategy chosen to . . .

   a.   Exploit a profit opportunity (which one)? _____
   b.   Remedy a competitive threat (which one)? _____
   c.   Capitalize on your strengths (which ones)? _____
        _____
   d.   Save money? _____
   e.   Other reasons?_____

   Why was this strategy chosen against your other <u>alternatives</u>?

5.   IMPLEMENTATION:

   a.   Who is responsible for implementing strategy? _____
   b.   When will that individual start?_____ Finish? _____
   c.   What <u>specifically</u> are the key tasks that need to be performed for the strategy to be implemented?

6.   REQUIRED SUPPORT FROM OTHER BANK DEPARTMENTS — What other areas need to provide support for implementation of strategy? (Specifically include Systems Development, Personnel, Operations, Marketing, Controller's and Loan Administration, when they apply.)

7.   GOALS — What are the specific <u>short-term</u> performance results you seek from implementation of this strategy?

Also to be taken into account, some manuals advise, is the necessity for maintaining a balance between the strategic goals and the resources — money, competence, facilities — available for accomplishment. Several of the planning guides also require the identification of the key risk factors and an analysis of their impact on the strategies selected.

The strategies most often asked for include product, marketing, manufacturing, competition, technology, financial resources, and management organization.

On a broad basis, one company suggests that strategies cover:

1. Competitive methods
2. Allocation of resources
3. Moves into new product or market areas
4. Acquisitions or divestments
5. Product and market extension requiring major investment and risk.

Often there are several alternative routes leading to the attainment of a particular objective and, before a strategy can be selected, the other routes must be explored. Although some companies do not require that this analysis be submitted to headquarters, other companies request the pros and cons of each alternative in order to evaluate the strategy recommended to accomplish the objective.

The strategy selected for each of the specified objectives defines the area of concentration to which the division has decided to devote its energies. Such decisions, of course, implicitly identify those areas which will be accorded a minimum of effort, or from which resources will be withheld altogether.

Because a division plan may generate many strategies, frequently the number that may be submitted is limited to those requiring the greatest commitment of resources or presenting the greatest risk. This is an attempt to discourage the submission of strategies that are of relatively minor significance to the overall corporate plan. (But at least one company asks for qualitative descriptions of programs that cannot be currently committed or quantified. Rather than omit them entirely because of the restriction on number, the instructions state, "Let us know what you are thinking.")

Strategies are usually thought of in terms of the market and competition, but they may cover other areas of corporate responsibility as well. This is evidenced by the fact that several companies ask for strategic plans from corporate staff units. The strategies of these units differ considerably from those of operating or line divisions. The planning guides that mention such requirements usually ask for the programs, projects and implementation plans pertaining to the support functions and services that staff units provide. The strategy plans may involve an assessment of the services provided within an area of responsibility and an evaluation of costs and benefits even though such estimates are difficult to quantify. One company, recognizing this, requires such an assessment from its staff units only every other year.

A tire and rubber producer requests a statement of strategic priorities, such as which of the staff unit's services should be emphasized. In a glass products manufacturer's manual, "competition" is defined for support divisions as "alternate ways of satisfying needs," such as consultants, purchased services, decentralization to divisions, etc. It further requests a listing of advantages and disadvantages for these alternatives in such areas as cost, service, security, quality, and so on.

Diversity of Strategies

Some of the previous strategies used for placing the corporation into a posture for achieving its growth and profitability objectives are included in one manual as an illustrative guide to divisional planners:

"Product lines or business segments, in a *loss position or at a very low profit level* (operating income at 5 percent or below of net capital employed), will have well-developed and high-confidence strategies which will show a return within a reasonable time period to an acceptable profitability rate, with full and realistic consideration being given to the new investment and management resources required. If this turnaround cannot be demonstrated, then they will be divested or eliminated in the most profitable manner possible. Divisions making divestments normally will be able to employ proceeds for reinvestment in growth emphasis businesses by increasing their capital budget.

"Those product lines early in their growth cycle, which are in a loss or low profit position, will be continued provided their future promise is substantial.

"Those current product lines or business segments that *do not have* a highly favorable combination of above-average market growth, competition limited and technical leadership characteristics, and have only moderate profit potential, *but which do generate acceptable cash flows, or are necessary to and supporting of other product lines or business segments* (excluding overhead considerations), will be put on a containment or harvest status. These businesses will be operated as efficiently as possible to maximize cash flow and new sales growth capital expenditures will be held to a minimum. Future strategies and plans should recognize and anticipate the possibility of future divestment or elimination and establish the optimum conditions for these actions."

— A tire and rubber producer

Action Programs

Action programs, operational plans and tactics are the specifics of the strategies developed. Where instructions for arriving at strategies may be imprecise, the documented requirements for action programs are more easily captured. A good many structured formats have been created that cover all the information needed at the corporate level for evaluating and making decisions on programs submitted (see Exhibits 32-36).

Action programs usually require data on most of the following elements:

- Description of program and/or objective
- Cost
- Results expected
- Time schedule or mileposts
- Assignment of responsibility
- Resource requirements

Other items that some firms also request are:

- Risk factors, or estimate of feasibility
- Cost-benefit analysis
- Priority of program
- Coordination required from other organization areas.

Other divisional input requested varies with the type of company and its businesses. Financial and other services organizations, for instance, usually ask for breakdowns on personnel projections, space requirements, and staff support figures.

Also, the amount of detail required often differs considerably between new development plans and those that implement an ongoing program.

Summaries of action plans are frequently wanted as an aid to top management for evaluation purposes. Establishing priorities for implementing strategies is eased, for example, when one-page summary forms are available, usually for each project submitted.

The implementation of strategies is another

(text continued on page 83)

Exhibit 32: Action Program Identification Form, with Illustrations — A Capital Goods, Automotive and Consumer Products Company

Forecast Data in <u>Thousands</u> of Constant
1974 <u>U.S. Dollars</u>
(Local Currency)

DIV./PLANT: <u>[name]</u>
PROGRAM NUMBER: <u>001</u>
PROGRAM RANKING: <u>I</u>   OF   <u>7</u>
TYPE OF PROGRAM: <u>Product Engineering</u>
PRODUCT LINE: <u>[name]</u>

TITLE: [Program Title]

OBJECTIVE AND SCOPE:
Standardize design of lever hoists marketed worldwide. Price the new design competitively while maintaining 20 percent net profit. New design will meet OSHA requirements and will be developed to metric standards. Project will require both division and corporate research center participation.

BUSINESS JUSTIFICATION:
Program will provide incremental sales of $388 in 1977 and $876 in 1979. Incremental profits in the same years will be $78 and $175. Return on incremental capital employed in the mature year will be 14 percent. Over a longer-term basis, [the company's] market share will continue to decline by about 1-2 percent per year unless this program providing for a redesign of the product line is approved.

INCREMENTAL INVESTMENT FORECASTS:

YEAR	CAPITAL REQUIREMENTS — ANNUAL	CAPITAL REQUIREMENTS — CUMULATIVE	PROGRAM EXPENSES — ANNUAL	PROGRAM EXPENSES — CUMULATIVE	QUARTERLY R AND D EXPENSE FORECAST — QUARTER	AMOUNT
Prior	$ –	$ –	$ –	$ 35	3/74	$ 20
1974	150	150	67	102	4/74	35
1975	53	203	25	127	1/75	17
1976	–	–	–	–	2/75	–
1977	–	–	–	–	3/75	–
1978	–	–	–	–	4/75	–
1979	–	–	–	–		
Beyond	–	–	–	–		

Probability of program success through capital spending   <u>90</u>   %
MATURE YEAR INCREMENTAL AVERAGE CAPITAL EMPLOYED: Net Plant and Equipment $ 177
  Working   100
  Total $ 277

INCREMENTAL (DECREMENTAL) SALES AND PROFIT:

FIRST YEAR OF INTRODUCTION <u>1975</u> ANTICIPATED SALES $ 75

	TARGET YEARS 1977 — SALES	1977 — PROFIT	TARGET YEARS 1979 — SALES	1979 — PROFIT	MATURE YEAR 1978 — SALES	1978 — PROFIT
ATTRITION PREVENTED	$ 95	$ 19	$ 246	$ 49	$ 150	$ 30
PRESENT PRODUCT INCREASE	395	79	882	176	583	117
NEW PRODUCT	–	–	–	–	–	–
COST REDUCTION	XX	–	XX	–	XX	–
TOTAL PRODUCT-LINE IMPACT	$ 490	$ 98	$1128	$ 225	$ 733	$ 147
CONFIDENCE OF SUCCESS	85%	80%	75%	70%	80%	75%
TOTAL AFTER DISCOUNTING FOR CONFIDENCE FACTOR	$ 368	$ 74	$ 846	$ 169	$ 550	$ 110
RETURN ON DISCOUNTED SALES	20 %		20 %		20 %	

MATURE YEAR RETURN ON INCREMENTAL AVERAGE CAPITAL EMPLOYED ....   40 %

_____   _____
GENERAL MANAGER   (DATE)   PROGRAM MANAGER   (DATE)

Exhibit 33: Action Program Summary Form — An Electrical Equipment Company

KEY STRATEGIC PROGRAM SUMMARY

_____ Division   Program Priority _____

Program Title:

_____

What major strategy is this program intended to implement?

Brief description of program.

_____

(Dollars in Thousands)

Total program costs, capital plus strategic managed costs $_____

Program completion date _____ ; DCF ROI:____% with TV;_____$ w/o TV.

Maximum cumulative negative cash flow $_____ will occur in 19____ .

Total 1975 SMC for this program as a % of total 1975 SMC for Division: _____%

Program Manager during 1975: _____

	PRIOR TO 1975	TOTAL PROGRAM	1975 PLAN
Program Costs:			
Related capital expenditures			
Total strategic managed costs			
Manufacturing			
Engineering			
Marketing			
Administration			
R and D			
Other			
Professional man-months required			
Program benefits:			
Incremental sales			
Incremental IAT			

Exhibit 33 (continued)

What are the main elements of uncertainty that might affect the planned results of this program?

What dates or program checkpoints have you set to measure satisfactory progress and resolution of uncertainties?

Is the required professional manpower already in place? If not, how many are to be added at your division and what fraction of the work will be accomplished for you by others?

Is this program to be funded in whole or in part by R and D? by another [company] division? by group or corporate funds? by an outside agency? If so, indicate the amount and nature of the support and the plans for achieving close coordination of actions.

Exhibit 34: Instructions for Program Summary — A Bank

A. DESCRIPTION (NATURE AND SCOPE)

This section should include a brief description by which you orient the reader to the program.

B. ACTIONS:

List in outline form the actions you will take to place the program into effect and obtain the results you list below. Remember, a program is a set of actions which will take you from your present capability to a higher capability; that is, how to produce a change. When you cease the change, cease the program.

For programming to be useful you must prearrange the actions the organization will take; therefore, they must be precise actions to which resources are assigned and with which a schedule can be associated. Actions should read: "Hire X people . . . , automate X processing . . . , promote X product with X dollars by . . . , prepare procedures manual for . . . , etc."

For large or complex programs such as acquisitions, new products, and automation applications, a supporting file of detailed actions will be necessary.

C. OBJECTIVES (RESULTS):

In this section you should provide the reader a definitive *estimate* of what the program will return to the bank or your organization in qualitative and quantitative terms. You should identify objectives which are a *result* of the program, not a list of the actions or steps of the program. You should use profit, revenue, lower costs, reduced risk, better morale, etc., as objectives. The objectives should be measurable or observable.

D. RESPONSIBILITIES (PROGRAM HEAD, OTHERS):

A program seldom proceeds on schedule or reaches its objectives without its assignment to a responsible manager. Likewise, collateral organizations must know what is expected of them.

E. SCHEDULE:

Goals or objectives without a date for attainment are virtually meaningless.

The planner can use a Gantt Chart to list the programmed actions and prepare a definitive schedule. More sophisticated scheduling techniques, such as PERT, are available through the Planning Officer.

F. REQUIRED RESOURCES (INDICATE WHETHER NEW OR REALLOCATED)

1. CAPITALIZED:

You should summarize the resources which the program requires. Here you list those which generally are, for accounting purposes, capitalized or written off over a number of years, such as equipment or buildings.

2. ASSETS OR LIABILITIES ASSIGNMENT:

A program may require little more than the reassignment of funds to a different asset category. Identify here the assignment or reassignment of assets and liabilities.

3. MANPOWER EXPENSES:

If you must hire or reassign personnel, make explicit here the numbers and types of people and the corresponding dollars of salary and fringe benefits.

4. OTHER EXPENSES:

All other outlays such as promotional costs, non-capitalized computer programming costs, interest costs, new office space, etc., should be noted here.

G. ANALYSIS:

1) For your own use, develop first a statement of the *economic* effects of the project. These effects include both benefits and costs, whether tangible or intangible. They also include a project's *independent* effects as well as its interdependent, interactive or "spillover" effects. The latter include possible repercussions of the project on (1) existing programs (or projects), and (2) proposed programs or projects. The distinction between *independent* and *interactive* is important. A program is truly independent if it has no conceivable effect on other cost and/or revenue activities of the

Exhibit 34 (continued)

bank, if it will neither increase nor decrease costs or benefits from either existing or currently proposed programs. The development of a branch in a new marketing area is an example of an opportunity that is conceivably independent in all major respects, while the introduction of a new savings account will obviously have potential interactive effects on existing account programs. 2) After determining economic effects, attention is directed toward their measurement. We must distinguish between benefits and costs and between tangibles and intangibles. Tangibles: to be measured in terms of dollar values. The benefits are cash *inflows* to the bank from fees, receipts and assorted revenues, salvage values, tax savings, and so forth, attributable to the project either directly or indirectly because of its spillover effects on existing programs. Costs are cash *outflows* from the bank, whether direct or indirect, due to the adoption of a project. It includes supplies, direct labor costs, taxes, equipment, etc. Previously incurred or sunk costs are excluded. One item which is not a cash outflow but which is nevertheless included in this category is the increase in net working capital that is caused by the project. Intangibles: to be described as clearly as possible. Note that we can distinguish between "apparent" and "true" intangibles. The former are those deemed to be intangibles because we have not reflected at length on how they may be measured and estimated, have neither consulted with those knowledgeable in the area nor looked at appropriate references. For example, the demand for a new service may be treated as an intangible simply because how one might estimate it is not apparent to the project sponsor. Yet there is a set of statistical sampling procedures involving carefully designed samples that can yield the required valuable information. Often an intangible is only apparent, not real. Another reason for labeling an effect an intangible is due to the failure to trace through, step-by-step, the logical process which produces the effect. To say that a new system will benefit the bank may be true but not very helpful. But to say, for example, that a new type of loan concept will appeal to customers with certain income, wealth, and other demographic characteristics, that there are so many such people in our marketing areas who will grow in number at a certain rate, and that preliminary testing suggests an annual net volume of X dollars (gross volume less the volume that would have been made anyway) enables one to come to grips with a tangible, incremental revenue estimate. (This is not to overlook the fact that if a concept is really successful, it will be initiated by competitors as soon as possible, limiting further the growth in incremental revenues). (3) Compute the net cash flows in each period. The net cash flow is the difference between the period's cash inflows and outflows. (4) Compute the realized internal rate of return and the net present value of the project.

Summary of Key Steps
Describe project; determine economic effects; measure benefits and costs, both direct and indirect, from the bank-as-a-whole point of view
    Tangible: express as cash inflow (benefits) and as cash outflows (costs)
    Intangible: describe clearly
. Compute net cash flows per period
. Compute realized internal rate of return and net present value
. Prepare Cost-Benefit Program Summary . . . .

H. RISK ANALYSIS:

Set forth the important events that can markedly change the expected performance of your proposal. This would include, for example, legal acts as well as competitor behavior, extraordinary changes in growth rates, marked changes in the regional economy, etc. Include both favorable as well as unfavorable events.

I. SUPPORTING FILES:

List here your supporting information by file number. The Cost-Benefit Program Summary Sheet is required when a program exceeds $100,000 in cash outflows and when a development project is to be submitted to the EDP Steering Committee.

J. AUDIT METHODS:

Here you should tell the reader when and how to observe the accomplishment of your objectives. You should define an audit method for your principal objectives. This can be done by defining an accounting and/or an information system that will cumulate the information bearing upon your objectives. You may even have to define an original report or set of observations for some objectives.

Exhibit 35: Action Program Summary Form, with Illustrations — A Paper Manufacturer

STRATEGIC ACTION PROGRAM SUMMARY

PROGRAM TITLE: Earnings improvement of the Y—Supplies Business
PROGRAM PURPOSE: Strengthen the profitability and defensibility of our position in the Y—Supplies market

STRATEGIC OBJECTIVES	STRATEGIES	TACTICAL GOALS	TACTICAL ACTIONS	RESOURCES REQUIRED	TARGET DATES BEGIN	END	RESPONSI-BILITY
1. Profitably commercialize new product YZ and achieve an annual sales rate of 1.5 million units by the end of 1978.	1. Introduce product YZ with a concentrated promotion campaign into the Southeastern region at a premium price.	Annual sales rate of 400,000 units in Southeastern region at a minimum price of $5 each by end of 1975.	Launch a 4-month, direct-mail campaign at city engineers of all cities with population of 5,000 or more.	$25,000 and 2 man-months	June 1, 1975	Sept. 30, 1975	Marketing Manager of Southeastern region
			Launch personal sales contact campaign at city engineers of all cities with 50,000 or more population.	$40,000 and 8 man-months	August 1, 1975	Nov. 1, 1975	Same
			Develop indirect sales channel by adding one distributor in Alabama and Georgia and two in South Carolina.	$100,000 cash investment for capital and 2 man-months	April, 1975	August, 1975	Same
			etc. other tactical actions, etc.				
	2. Build a small initial plant in Birmingham with 1 million-unit capacity which can be doubled in capacity to 2 million units in 1977 if the market sustains a growth rate of 10% or more through 1976.	Construct original 1 million-unit plant within total cost budget of $1.3 million.	Use turnkey contract for speedy design and construction of the plant. Specify the X-11 vacuum molding process in the design of equipment.	$1,300,000 and 20 man-months	January 1, 1975	Aug. 15, 1975	Project Manager
		Start up initial new plant and achieve a direct unit cost under continuous operation of $1.50 per unit by the end of September, 1975.	Complete training program of key personnel prior to completion of construction. Other tactical actions, . . . etc., . . .	$50,000 and 15 man-months	May 1, 1975	Aug. 1, 1975	Plant Manager
2. Upgrade quality of products Y9 through Y15 and their acceptance in the market while increasing our average Y-gross-margin to 35% by the end of 1976.	1. Reorganize the purchasing department. . .and so forth. . .	Reduce spoilage in raw material. . .and so forth. . .	Use national account purchasing as leverage for. . .and so forth. . .				

Exhibit 36: Action Program Summary Form — A Glass Products Manufacturer

DIVISION _____

OBJECTIVE _____

TASK DESCRIPTION: One or two sentences describing
                           the nature of the task.

COSTS:

	1974	1975	1976
Expense	_____	_____	_____
Capital	_____	_____	_____
Manpower	_____	_____	_____

BENEFITS: A brief statement (quantified where
                   possible) describing the benefits or value
                   of the task.

TASK MILESTONES

	Completion Date	Description	Responsibility
1.			
2.			
3.			
4.			
5.			

Final Completion Date _____

Overall Responsibility _____

place in the planning process where volume must be held down. Enthusiastic managers may submit programs for every aspect of the strategy, burdening an already voluminous compilation with action plans of relatively minor significance. This is why, for instance, one company asks for "only those 10 percent of major actions that will have 80 percent impact on earnings objectives." Another asks for "only those activities that are significantly different from normal day-to-day operations."

Contingency Planning, Alternative Plans, and Scenarios

The present certainty of greater future uncertainties has drawn the interest of many companies to contingency planning. (Some guides refer to this type of planning as "supplemental planning" or "alternative planning," but it should not be confused with "alternative strategies," discussed earlier.)

Contingency planning, in the words of one company participating in this study, is "a planned reaction to a short-term or long-term diverse condition which threatens the attainment of profit performance agreed upon. The objective of our contingency planning will be to minimize any negative variation from planned performance."

Although most of the planners interviewed said that they were looking into contingency planning and scenario-type exercises, formal guides for such plans are not much in evidence in the manuals and other documents submitted for this study.

The reluctance to build contingency planning into corporate requirements is based on several considerations, primarily its effects on managers.[1] Requiring contingency plans in addition to basic plans may overburden a manager's already considerable planning responsibilities. Because long-range planning is such a demanding

---

[1] Contingency planning projects are carried out at the corporate level, according to several of the planning executives interviewed, generally on a task force or ad hoc basis. They are usually confidential, both for morale purposes and to preserve the elements of surprise and secrecy.

effort in itself, some planning directors believe that increasing it could easily lead to a downward delegation of the function, and the formulation of plans by a lower echelon — a potentially worthless effort. It is also felt that a manager's motivation toward the basic plan may be lessened if he feels there is another plan "waiting in the wings."

Also "contingency planning" has acquired a negative connotation in management terminology, and the adverse effect on managerial morale must be weighed. (This is true despite the fact that some guides point out that contingency planning may provide for opportunities advantageous to the organization.)

In some companies alternative plans are requested only from "some units" in the organization. This too, of course, accounts for the absence of corporate guidelines on this subject.

What appears to be a common practice at present in the area of contingency planning is for the corporate level to issue or to request high and low scenarios, or best- and worst-possible cases. These, of course, are in addition to "most likely" or "expected" cases. Banks, for example, frequently ask for scenarios based on higher and lower interest rates; heavily regulated industries may call for scenarios based on the enactment of new or changed legislation.

"Discussion" is invited on these projections, including consideration of the factors that would affect the long-range plan or the factors that would effect changes in the key assumptions. "What if . . .?" questions by the divisions are encouraged. Full financial implications or detailed strategies are rarely required.

Many of these practices apply currently only to short-range operational or annual budget plans. In the latter case, for instance, one company calls for "profit models" reflecting revenue at 110 percent, 100 percent, 90 percent and 80 percent of plan. Some planners caution that introducing several variables or scenarios for a number of divisions may invite too many contingency plans.

Several companies in this study try to present the rationale of the contingency planning exercises they are undertaking to their managers.

Exhibit 37: Guide to Contingency Planning — A Diversified Industrial Manufacturing Company

---

SUPPLEMENTAL PLANNING

Up to this point, all your efforts have been based on what you view as the most likely set of events in the future. We now wish you to release the constraints on the plan and develop the situation in which all good things imaginable occur (i.e., "everything going right"). This will permit you to place an upper boundary on your division's activities while expressing to management what might be achieved if desired resources were available.

In order that we do not overstate the optimistic side of the plan, you are also requested to establish a lower boundary. . . . . This situation will reflect the catastrophic consequences of all bad things imaginable (i.e., "everything going wrong"). This activity ensures proper realism within the plan while preventing the ultimate error of a totally unforeseen emergency. Thus your pessimistic plan will become an insurance policy below which you are confident operating results will not fall.

Your optimistic and pessimistic plans should take the following abbreviated format:

1) A summary financial presentation detailing the expected results of each case. These results will be indicated through projections of net sales, pretax profit, ROI, and cash flow.

2) A brief write-up highlighting the circumstances that would yield these results.

3) A statement of the chance that this set of events will occur. This statement will be presented through a single probability (e.g., two percent indicating the likelihood that this situation will become a reality).

One aerospace components company that requests alternative plans from its subsidiaries explains that: "The basic plan will be used in the financial consolidation and in the discussions with the parent company. The alternative plans, however, will aid the parent company in long-range strategic and financial planning in the event critical assumptions do not materialize as forecast."

In explaining its instructions for contingency plans, a paper company notes:

"Obviously, no meaningful business plan ever totally occurs. There will always be some critical things within the plan that happen other than as assumed. A contingency plan for a particular eventuality establishes actions to be taken in advance of the possible occurrence, and in the event of the actual occurrence. These actions will enable the business unit to mitigate the effects of unfavorable variations, and capitalize fully on favorable variations. In other words, contingency plans are intended to minimize downside risk and maximize upside potential. By having taken the advance actions, and having

the contingent actions 'on the shelf,' the response time for dealing with variations is shortened, and the effectiveness of implementation is improved."

The letter from a company president introducing a recent planning cycle states: "Inflation, shortages, monetary instability, record interest rates, an uncertain economic outlook, and the possibility of a recession — all these, and more, highlight the necessity for well-thought-out contingency planning."

References to or directions for this type of planning usually are presented under the guidelines for formulating strategy. They are, for the most part, presented simply and without much elaboration. Here are some typical examples:

"In your discussion of contingencies identify the key contingent events that could affect your strategic plan, and cover the following questions: To what extent would such events require modification of the goals, strategies and programs you've outlined? What steps are you taking to deal with the uncertain nature of these events and their impact upon your business, should they occur?"

* * *

"Due to uncertainties surrounding the initial case environmental forecast, especially crude [oil] prices net of taxation and the economic environment, some divisions may wish to test their strategies and programs against alternative environments. Others will be given alternative environments against which project economics may be tested."

* * *

". . . There should be a discussion of possible opportunities or risks which may occur, the impact these occurrences could potentially have on the financial results, and the contingency plans which the operating unit has should they occur."

* * *

"If a [business unit] has identified major alternative or contingency strategies, it should include a second set of order-of-magnitude financial projections to indicate the potential impact of the strategy on the business."

* * *

"What is our risk in following each of the alternate strategies? . . . What would be the impact of failure? . . . What early warning do we have? What is our contingency plan?"

Exhibit 38: Guide to Contingency Planning — A Paper Company

CONTINGENCY PLANS

The list of possible occurrences for which contingency plans are developed should contain, at minimum, favorable and/or unfavorable variations in those items on the Critical Actions and Events Summary. In addition, the business unit should select other items from its Strategic and Operating Action Programs for contingency plan development for which the consequences of variation would be serious.

The elements of a contingency plan are as follows:

1.	Occurrence	— The action or event at variance with that assumed in the expected plan. E.g., "The availability of SBR polymer at reasonable prices will not enable us to satisfy the demand for stereopticons."
2.	Chance	— The estimated probability that the occurrence will happen. E.g., "25 percent."
3.	Trigger	— A signal that will be used to conclude that the occurrence is about to happen. E.g., "Judgment of Purchasing Department based on contacts with two key suppliers."
4.	Advance actions	— Those actions to be taken prior to the trigger in order to reduce reaction time. E.g., "Develop alternative compounds, using readily available polymers, which meet stereopticon specifications."
5.	Contingent actions	— Those actions to be taken only in the event of the trigger. E.g., "Launch Technical Service program to assure sales force and customer of continued stereopticon quality."
6.	Financial impact	— The approximate incremental impact of the occurrence on the business unit's sales and earnings during the first year of the plan, assuming that the advance and contingent actions are taken.

Exhibit 38 (continued)

The financial impact, the approximate variance from the expected plan, may be difficult to estimate if the occurrence is one of degree. For example, the duration of a strike, the amount of a competitive price cut, or the length of delay in a new product commercialization program, have to be specified before the financial consequences can be approximated. In such cases, it is useful to ask: "Assuming that the occurrence does happen, to what degree would I expect it to happen?"

Contingency plans are to be broken into two parts: "optimistic," containing those occurrences that would have a favorable impact on the first year's earnings, and "pessimistic," containing the occurrences resulting in lower earnings. The forms on the following pages are to be used to document the business unit's contingency plans.

In order to provide an indication of the range of uncertainty of the first year's financial results, the business unit's sales and earnings must be estimated under both an "optimistic" and a "pessimistic" case. This information is to be provided in the following format:

	Net Sales ($000)	Earnings BT ($000)
Optimistic Case		
Expected Case		
Pessimistic Case		

The "expected" case will correspond exactly to the first year's sales and earnings data in the Profile System and Operating Budget.

The "optimistic" case data represent a set of "upside" results that the business unit feels have a 25 percent chance of being achieved or exceeded. Similarly, the "pessimistic" case presents a set of "downside" results. In essence, the unit says, "There is a 25 percent chance that the actual outcome will be the 'pessimistic' case or worse."

The contingency plans provide one set of inputs to the estimation of this range of uncertainty. In reality, of course, the actual variation from the expected case will be caused by several relatively minor occurrences in addition to the critical actions and events dealt with in the contingency plans. Consequently, such factors as fluctuations in projected sales price, volumes, materials costs, etc., ought to be considered in establishing these ranges of expected performance. However, it is not recommended that the business unit attempt to statistically compute the optimistic and pessimistic cases on the basis of the probabilities and financial impacts in the contingency plans.

Exhibit 38 (continued)

CONTINGENCY PLANS

☒ OPTIMISTIC ☐ PESSIMISTIC

OCCURRENCE	CHANCE	TRIGGER	ADVANCE ACTIONS / CONTINGENT ACTIONS	FINANCIAL IMPACT	
				NET SALES ($000)	EARNINGS BT ($000)
IPM Corp. has major prolonged strike starting about August 1.	25%	IPM's labor relations have not substantially improved by July 1.	**Advance Actions** Increase inventory in matching and higher quality lines. (Invest $35,000.) Develop promotion campaign and advertising literature aimed at competitive issues of reliable delivery and quality of product. Develop incentives for customer to sign new long-term contract. **Contingent Actions** Offer price concessions on matching lines. Launch promotion and advertising campaigns. Initiate biweekly sales meetings to coordinate new accounts efforts.	2,000	500
The General Corp. will attempt new national accounts direct sales program.	33%	They begin servicing their Imperial Food Chain and Ford accounts with direct sales.	**Advance Actions** In February, launch advertising campaign in trade publications stressing long-term loyalty to independent distributors. In March, launch campaign at large accounts emphasizing rush order service from local distributors. Finance inventory increases at our distributors under guise of economics in distribution. (Invest $20,000.) **Contingent Actions** Initiate missionary sales campaign at medium-sized accounts to assist in taking advantage of competing distributor's letdown. Allow distributor's price concessions to reduce inventory and gain new accounts. Introduce new product-V15 through distributors within 2 months rather than through direct sales.	1,000	200

Exhibit 38 (continued)

☐ OPTIMISTIC ☒ PESSIMISTIC

OCCURRENCE	CHANCE	TRIGGER	ADVANCE ACTIONS / CONTINGENT ACTIONS	FINANCIAL IMPACT — NET SALES	FINANCIAL IMPACT — EARNINGS BT ($000)
J. S. Seagull Corp. introduces YZ into Southeastern markets during Spring.	20%	Seagull issues contract for production of YZ prior to June 1.	**Advance Actions** Build inventory of black dye materials required for production of Super-YZ. Complete by May 1. ($20,000 investment.) Develop standby promotion campaign for commercialization of Super-YZ. Complete plans by May 1. **Contingent Actions** Drop commercialization of YZ. Accelerate commercialization of Super-YZ. Modify the vacuum molding process to a vacuum extrusion process. Launch standby promotion campaign in lieu of planned campaign.	(1,000)	(150)
Fuel gas supply interrupted at Birmingham plant.	30%	Notice from Gas Company.	**Advance Actions** Complete construction of reserve oil tanks by March 1 ($30,000 investment). Locate and contract for oil supply by Feb. 1. Fill tanks by April 1 ($45,000 investment). **Contingent Actions** Switch to fuel oil from new reserve tanks.		
The small Lowline Corp. cuts prices at least 10% on Product Y5.	30%	Lowline announces price cut on Y5.	**Advance Actions** Increase our inventory of the higher quality Y8 to 25% above normal ($50,000 investment). Develop standby promotional literature designed to emphasize false economy of switching to lower quality and the availability advantages of buying from larger corporation. **Contingent Actions** Immediately allow matching price reductions on our superior Y8 and launch promotion campaign.		(100)

Exhibit 39: Guide to Contingency Planning — A Tire Manufacturer

INTRODUCTION

A contingency, by definition, is some future event which could happen but which is not anticipated in the regular planning process. Contingencies can result in a positive or negative effect on a business. [The company] and division plans are based on the most probable turn of events, and separate contingency plans can be developed for unusual situations which are not anticipated in the regular plan, but which could occur and which would have major impact.

An economic downturn is probably the most important contingency for [the company] to consider. There are, however, many other events, not included in regular planning, which could have a major impact and warrant a contingency plan which could be implemented should the unplanned-for event occur.

GUIDELINE FOR CONTINGENCY PLANNING

1. Identify the major developments which could happen that would have major impact on the business.

   The development could be broad and affect many aspects of many businesses such as a downturn in the U.S. economy. It could, however, be narrower and affect only one business or even only part of a business. Examples are: a lowered tariff on imports, a strike, a raw material shortage, a change in competition, a major change in design, manufacturing or material technology.

2. Evaluate the relative significance of each potential development and the likely effects. This evaluation should consider:

   a. An estimate of the probability of the development happening and the frequency with which it might happen.

   b. The impact on the business and whether or not it will be a short-time impact, continuing or something in between.

3. After having identified those developments which would warrant contingency planning, develop a plan of action which should include:

   a. The objectives.

   b. The strategy for achieving the objectives.

   c. The plan of implementation.

4. A good time to consider the need for contingency plans is during the preparation of short- and long-term plans. A good time to do the contingency plan is after completing the short- or long-term plan.

CHECKLIST FOR CONTINGENCY PLANNING FOR ECONOMIC DOWNTURN

A. IDENTIFYING THE APPROACH OF AN ECONOMIC DOWNTURN

   1. External Reports.

      a. Economic indicators distributed by various major publications and reporting services on a daily, weekly or monthly basis that show:

      (1) Broad industry or market figures of national scope:

         (a) sales, prices and price indexes
         (b) unit production and production indexes
         (c) employment and unemployment
         (d) corporate profits
         (e) construction starts
         (f) Investments in R and D and capital expansion
         (g) inventories

Exhibit 39 (continued)

    (2) Financial figures on:

        (a) investment credit
        (b) consumer spending
        (c) various price indexes and averages on common stock
        (d) prime interest rate

  b. Economic indicators distributed by national publications and reporting services from individual trade associations and agencies of the local, state or Federal Government that focus on a specific industry, market or product. The data presented are similar to one or more of the subjects listed in a. (1) above.

  c. Other useful reports stem from:

    (1) corporate office
    (2) other [company] divisions
    (3) personal contacts; banks, clubs, etc.

2. Internal Reports

  a. Written or verbal reports on present and expected product demand in the marketplace (i.e., from field salesmen or management visits into the field, etc.)

  b. Number of inquiries and frequency of orders resulting.

  c. Trends in incoming orders, shipments and backlog.

  d. Trends in competitive pricing.

3. Comparison of External and Internal Reports

A comparison of external and internal data should identify the downturn as being national, divisional or both, and provide a basis for determining the extent of the downturn, the actions to be taken, and the timing.

B. ACTIONS TO AVERT MOST OF THE NEGATIVE INFLUENCE OF AN ECONOMIC DOWNTURN

1. General

  a. Know all major fixed and variable costs. Make certain break-even calculations and charts are available and up-to-date.

  b. Determine which operating costs are necessary (minimum costs) and which are optional.

  c. Tighten financial controls and increase their report frequency.

  d. Categorize products, projects, procedures and personnel in order of expendability.

  e. Estimate timing for priority of action against the severity of a downturn; implement by phase.

  f. Communicate the business conditions and make certain those communicated with (key managers, department heads, etc.) do the same.

  g. Make the responsibility for actions to be taken crystal clear.

2. Specific

All costs involved in marketing, manufacturing and administration should be reduced to necessary (minimum) and optional costs identified with priority of need. The cost determinations plus a determination of the utility and/or performance of these three major business functions should result in a clear-cut course of action.

Exhibit 39 (continued)

a. Marketing — This function of a business is directly responsible for generating most of the revenue. It also generates great cost. Its key aspects of sales, service, advertising and promotion, and distribution can be scrutinized quickly and closely per the following checklist:

(1) Sales — A sales force that is inefficient wastes the money a company already has. If it is not proficient, it does not earn the money (sales) a company wants; hence, the sales function is extremely important in managing a company in both good and bad economic times and should be analyzed first, in most cases, in the event of an impending economic downturn.

    (a)   Sales management, staff and office help (home and field offices).
    (b)   Direct field sales versus representatives.
    (c)   Customer and technical service.
    (d)   Product or project manager group.
    (e)   Product-line profitability.
    (f)   Possible long-term sales commitments.
    (g)   Possible acceptance of volume business with lower than normal gross margin.

(2) Advertising and Promotion

    (a)   Management and staff.
    (b)   Advertising and promotion alternatives, i.e., black and white versus color; frequency and size of space advertising; new brochures really needed?
    (c)   Possible conversion of some advertising and promotion moneys to new products.
    (d)   Trade shows and conventions; conversion of moneys to quicker return projects?
    (e)   In-house work versus agency work and vice versa.

(3) Distribution

    (a)   Management and staff.
    (b)   Owned versus leased trucks versus common carrier.
    (c)   Warehouse.
    (d)   Inventory control.

b. Manufacturing

(1) Management, staff, line supervision and production workers.
(2) Quality control and scrap control.
(3) Value analysis; materials control (with Purchasing Department).
(4) Greater emphasis on cost reduction, especially the type with immediate results even if only one-time rather than continuing savings.
(5) Direct and indirect labor cost analysis for possible reduction.
(6) Productivity analysis for possible unit cost reduction.
(7) Consider short workweek instead of layoffs (after deadwood gone) in order to maintain the nucleus of a trained work force.
(8) Expand plant capacity, if necessary, in small increments.

c. Administration

(1) Management and staff; flexibility is the key; use outside services and manpower for essential one-time projects rather than commit long-term by hiring new employees.

(2) Tighten requirements and/or approvals on:

    (a)   New hires (freeze total number at certain point).
    (b)   Expenses above budget or not budgeted.

Exhibit 39 (continued)

        (c)   Purchase commitments; avoid long-term.
        (d)   Inventory.
        (e)   Administrative travel.
        (f)   Overtime.
        (g)   Nonessential projects.
        (h)   Capital expenditures.

(3)   Examine paperwork channels for possible streamline.

(4)   Identify marginal aspects of the business and reduce or eliminate according to the duration and severity of the economic downturn.

(5)   Convert fixed expenses to variable as much as possible and practical.

(6)   Make certain R and D, engineering and product development departments are effective and efficient.

(7)   Make certain all department heads and, in turn, their people know and understand the economic situation.

(8)   Computer utilization; cost and alternatives.

Appendix

Tables of Contents of Planning Manuals and Sample Plan Outlines

9. Planning Timetables
   A. General
   B. Strategic Planning Timetable
   C. Financial Planning Timetable

10. Glossary

Table of Contents – A Recreational Products Company

1. Purpose of Guide
2. Purpose of Strategic Plan
3. Strategic Planning Process

    3.1 Definition of Terms
    Key Objectives
    Strategies
    Major Action Programs
    Major Product Lines

    3.2 Strategic Planning Process
    Evaluation of Present Position
    Forecast of Changes
    Setting of Key Objectives
    Formulation of Strategies
    Definition of Action Programs
    Projection of Financial Results

    3.3 Development of [The company's]
    Strategic Plan – *Changes in 1974*
    Summary of the Changes
    Executive Office Objectives
    and Guidelines
    Units with No Executive Office
    Objectives and Guidelines
    Specific Changes for 1974

    3.4 Use of Common Economic Forecasts –
    Coordination with Senior Area
    Representatives

    3.5 Coordination of Strategic Plan

    3.6 Reporting Location Units

4. Financial Information Required

    4.1 General Guidelines

    4.2 Standardized Financial Information
    and Forms

    4.3 Data to be Submitted with
    the Budget

    4.4 Compound Growth Rate Examples
    and Table

    4.5 List of Forms to be Used with
    Samples

5. Response to Executive Office
   Objectives

    Justification for Non-
    concurrence
    Comments on Specific Issues

6. Group Strategic Plan

    6.1 Outline of Written Submission

    6.2 Scope of Content
    Summary of Significant
    Changes
    Assessment of Critical Issues in
    Business Unit Plans
    Major Group Strategies and
    Action Programs
    Diversification Plan
    Financial Forecasts

    6.3 Operations Management Board
    Presentation Format and Sample
    View Graphs

7. Business Unit Strategic Plan

    7.1 Outline of Written Submission

    7.2 Scope of Content
    Key Objectives – Rationale
    Situation Analysis
    Rationale for the Major
    Product Line Objectives and Market
    Share Targets
    Business Unit and Major Product
    Line Strategies and Action
    Programs
    Product Line Schedules
    Manufacturing Plan

    7.3 Industrial Product Marketing Plans
    Situation Analysis
    Business Unit and Major Product
    Line Strategies and Action
    Programs

7.4 Operations Management Board Presentation Format and Sample View Graphs

8. Submissions Required

8.1 General Procedure and Sequence of Events

8.2 Distribution

8.3 Submission Schedule

8.4 Business Units and Their Categories

8.5 List of Major Product Lines

8.6 Strategic Plan Presentation Requirements by Group and Business Unit

9. Economic Forecasts

9.1 Definition of Economic Terms

9.2 Long-Term Forecast — United States

Sample Contents of a Five-Year Plan — A Financial Services Firm

1. Brief description of business charter.
2. Assessment of current year's business performance.
3. General description of external factors affecting your business in 1973–1977. (Note: This is in addition to environmental assumptions issued by Corporate Planning Department.)
4. Discussion of competition, and comparison with your operation.
5. Statement of your goals and strategies.
6. Total estimate of market and your planned share of market.
7. Development of new products for markets internally or through acquisition.
8. Critical issues and problems confronting business.
9. Planned programs and actions.
10. Financial schedules: past years and projected five years.
11. Capital requirements.
12. Taxes.
13. Manpower and space requirements.

Sample Outline of Operating Company Business Plan — A Food Processor

I. *Review of Progress Against Previous Plan:* Financial results and progress on action programs.

II. *General Planning Assumptions:* Analysis, research, market studies, and overall business intelligence carried out by the operating company's management team will provide a body of information from which management draws certain conclusions regarding its external and internal environments.

A. *Economic and Competitive Environment (External)*

The purpose of this section is to describe the outside environmental influences that may affect the company's business while stressing their implications. Management's thorough analysis of all pertinent factors is an essential part of sound planning. A lengthy discussion of these factors is not necessary. Focus should be on the major *assumptions* that company management draws from its analyses of economic and social trends and competitive pressures which provide the rationale for major business decisions on priorities, strategies and goals.

Among the many factors *to be considered* are the following:

Demographic

• Population growth, age, trends, income segments.

• National income data: gross national product, inflationary trends, balance of payments, unemployment.

• Purchasing power and the nature of demand.

• National economic and educational developments and changes.

• Trends in government regulations, taxes, controls, attitude toward business.

• Family formations, sizes, characteristics.

Demand/Market/Competitive Factors

• Rate of growth in market demand for our product lines; products that show declining trends.

- Major product competitors (old and new) and any significant competitive threats or changes in their shares, strategy, policies, etc.
- Eating habits (in home and away), types of meals and foods consumed, maid service, shopping habits, price/quality sensitivity.
- Other consumer trends which may create problems and opportunities for established and/ or new businesses.
- Industry merger, acquisitions and vertical integration activity.
- Any major changes in distribution channels, pricing, raw material costs, distributor relations, customer policies that would affect business strategy.
- Major industry technological changes in production, processing, R and D, and the like that affect the competitive nature of the business environment.

Processed Foods Industry
- Growth rates
- Fastest-growing product segments
- Price levels
- Distribution channels
- Competitive forces
- Portion of total national expenditures

B. *Company's Present Position*

The previous section focused on external forces at work that affect the company's growth. This section is devoted to a summary of the *internal* situation of the company, its present position in the businesses in which it operates, and a review of its competitive strengths and weaknesses.

Again, the stress is on the significant factors which influence future growth rather than simply a review of historical trends. One way to think about the organization of this section is in terms of a business audit or status report regarding the major functional areas and relative company strengths and weaknesses.

Competitive Situation of Company's Major Product Groups

- Market shares and trends
- Consumer franchise: awareness, interest, loyalty, purchase habits, etc.

- Advantages and disadvantages of ours vs. competitors'
- Margins: company's; trade's

Profitability (of each major product group)
- Product contribution
- Operating income

R and D Effort
- Strategy
- Spending plans
- Line extensions vs. "new" product development
- Professional manpower strengths and requirements

Financial Management
- Cash management
- Accounts receivable
- Inventories
- Utilization of fixed assets

Cost Reduction Needs and Opportunities
- Absolute dollars (or local currency)
- Percent of total company profits
- Return-on-investment

Management/Organization
- Strengths and weaknesses
- Recruiting, development needs
- Future organization and manpower requirements

Employees
- Total number and trends
- Average sales per employee
- Size of sales force
- Technological scientists and engineers as percentage of all employees

C. *Summary: Major Problems, Issues and Priorities*

- What major problems confront management?
- What important competitive threats must be coped with?
- What significant improvement opportunities can be identified?
  - Different marketing strategies?

— Product-line extensions?

— "New-to-[the company]" product development and introductions?

— Development of new markets?

— Price increases?

• What significant improvement opportunities can be identified?

— Production, administration, distribution cost reductions?

— Computer utilization, systems research, data processing?

— Manufacturing and processing technique?

— Sales, supervisory, management effectiveness?

— Disposal of unnecessary facilities?

• What priorities do you attach to these opportunities?

— What are critical and must be resolved immediately?

— What can be postponed? For how long?

• What assistance will be required from headquarters?

— Financial

— Temporary staff assistance

— Longer-term "loans" of people

— Other

III. *Company Objectives and Strategies:* Based on the major planning assumptions, summarize the emphasis management places on each of the five possible growth areas and the particular strategy and goals (if any) for each:

• Expand present business
• Develop "new" business
• Acquisitions
• Cost reduction
• Financial management

A. *Checklist for Development of Growth Strategy and Business Objectives:*

Who are the basic customers for your products?

• Housewife, all women, entire family, any person?

• What attractive growth opportunities are there for our company?

• On which can you capitalize (longer-term) with available (or attainable) financial, physical, technological and human resources?

Processed Foods Industry

• Fastest growing segments
• Most profitable segments
• What areas are we in?
• What areas should we — or can we — get in?

Potential "Food" Markets

• Frozen foods
• Snack foods
• Breakfast foods
• Beverages
• Institutional
• Pet foods
• New processes

Other Food and Food-Channel Areas

• Fastest-growing segments
• Most profitable segments
• What areas offer attractive diversification opportunities?

Trade with Other [Corporate] Companies

• Sales possibilities
• Interchange of product, R and D, and other ideas
• Cost-reduction possibilities
• Steps required
• Problems to be resolved

All of the above represent a sample of the type of prethinking that management must do as part of the business planning effort. In reviewing these areas with higher management, the emphasis should be on summarizing (not detailing) the major assumptions and conclusions drawn. Such a summary would provide the necessary background to understand the plan itself which follows.

IV. *Existing Business Optimization:* Based on the analysis of priorities, needs and opportunities, summarize the *highlights* of the optimization plan for the *existing* business.

• Major strategy and goals for each product group.

• Product needs (present line and new requirements).

• Marketing spending strategies.

• New and unique merchandising and promotion programs.

• Planning for increased margins.

• Any other major programs or studies designed to improve sales, distribution, share-of-market, trade interest, consumer acceptance.

• New business development via new markets.

• Cost reduction, process improvement, other needs to ensure attainment of profit goals.

V. *New Business Development:* Having discussed the existing business, summarize the plans for expanding the business in the years ahead through diversification, acquisition, export and any other methods.

• Which new markets are attractive: short- and long-term?

• What is best way to enter: new product development or acquisition?

• What is acquisition policy, criteria, candidates (if any)?

• What is strategy for developing "new-to-[the company]" products?

• What is investment strategy in the "new business" area?

• What are goals and timetables?

Against the short- and long-term plans for the growth of the existing business and the addition of new business, the plans for other functional areas can be developed.

VI. *Operations:* In relation to business growth goals summarize (for production, R and D, purchasing, warehousing and distribution) the leading priorities and major plans covering:

• Increased efficiencies and reduced costs.

• Improved processes.

• Product quality, improvements, developments.

• R and D strategy, spending, activities planning.

• Other?

VII. *Organization, Management/Planning/ Management Development:* Considering nature of immediate improvement opportunities and business goals for years ahead, discuss the organization and management improvements that will be required — for each functional division and for company overall:

• Anticipated organizational changes to manage future business.

• Projection of management needs: numbers, types, skills, etc.

• Backup strength for key managerial positions.

• Management-development needs tailored to present and future organization.

• Recruiting, training, compensation requirements over next five years.

• Steps to take, timing; help needed.

VIII. *Financial Management:* Against improvement opportunities identified and financial resources required, describe major priorities and programs with respect to:

• Improved financial management (cash management, accounts receivable, inventories, leasing, borrowing, taxes, etc.)

• Increased utilization and productivity of fixed assets.

• Major changes in sources and uses of funds.

• Strategy for financing acquisition and other business development activities.

• Contribution to cost-reduction projects.

IX. *Financial Summary:* The standard format included in the guidance section of this booklet must be used by every affiliate to assure uniform treatment of financial information. The form of presentation of any additional financial information can be determined by the individual affiliate.